The Delusions of Invulnerability

CLASSICAL INTER/FACES

Series editors: Susanna Braund and Paul Cartledge

Also available

THE DELUSIONS OF INVULNERABILITY

Wisdom and Morality in Ancient
Greece, China and Today

G.E.R. Lloyd

Duckworth

First published in 2005 by
Gerald Duckworth & Co. Ltd.
90-93 Cowcross Street
London EC1M 6BF
Tel: 020 7490 7300
Fax: 020 7490 0080
inquiries@duckworth-publishers.co.uk
www.ducknet.co.uk

A catalogue record for this book is available
from the British Library

ISBN 0 7156 3386 4

Typeset by e-type, Liverpool
Printed and bound by
CPI Bath

Contents

Preface

The ancient and the modern worlds seem poles apart, and from the point of view of the material circumstances of many people's existence, they are. But a number of fundamental questions, concerning what makes life worth living, and how social and political relations are best organised, were debated in such civilisations as ancient Greece and China and the answers that were given are worth reviewing for the light they can shed on the problems we continue to face today. Of course not everyone in such ancient societies formulated views on such matters, and this raises a further set of questions as to how those who did saw their own role. How did individuals carve out a niche for themselves to take up positions on basic questions of values and ideals? Whom were they hoping to persuade, and how did they set about doing so?

The strategic aim of this book is to explore what we can learn from the ancient world on questions that continue to haunt us today. My tactics are to begin, in the first three chapters, with issues to do with the constitution, organisation, internal rivalries, self-image and public face, of learned elites. How were different traditions of learning developed? Where do they resemble or differ from the various styles of 'philosophy' we can exemplify in the modern world? Are our ideas and practices concerning the recruitment to, and accountability of, elite groups – such as 'philosophers' or 'scientists' – appropriate to the ends and functions they should serve? What can we gather from ancient communication practices – with audiences of different types – that may throw light on modern ones? I concentrate, in these studies, on ancient Greece and China, but broaden my inquiry, where opportunities present themselves, to other ancient and pre-modern societies, notably Mesopotamia.

In the final three chapters I turn to the question of ideals. I examine first ancient, and modern, preoccupations with attempts to

7

make life somehow secure from misfortune – to achieve invulnerability, no less. I probe the difficulties that societies have always found in ensuring just and equitable relations between individuals and groups, and with other societies, whether powerful or weak. Finally I reflect, from a modern perspective, on the various exemplary models for living that have been proposed in ancient civilisations.

In all six studies I investigate ancient societies not just for their own sakes, but to draw out lessons from their experience that bear on our own ongoing, contemporary, problems. My inquiry has been driven, throughout, by the conviction that research into the ancient world can provide a precious resource for our own self-understanding.

Earlier versions of some of the materials in this book have been presented at seminars in Paris, Lille and Washington D.C. I am grateful to my hosts on those occasions, Professors Christian Jacob, André Laks and Gregory Nagy, and to my audiences, for their constructive comments, while absolving them, as is customary, for the shortcomings that remain.

G.E.R.L.

1

The Pluralism of Philosophical Traditions

One of the striking features of intellectual life in the last hundred years or so is the way in which quite diverse traditions of philosophy have been cultivated in different countries. That is true even within different European countries, before we go any further afield, say to North America, let alone to India, or to what is still often sweepingly referred to as 'the Far East'.

This is not just a matter of the particular fads and fashions cultivated in the philosophical journals in different languages: it is a matter also of what counts as 'philosophy', of the way it is taught, the basic curricula of departments of philosophy in the universities. To speak personally, for a moment, in the Cambridge of the early 1950s, where I received my philosophical formation, almost no attention was paid, in the Faculty of Moral Sciences (as it was then known), to large areas of continental philosophy, including phenomenology and even existentialism. True, some reference to Sartre was made in the *English* faculty, for they ran a paper called 'The English Moralists', which began, astonishingly, with Plato and Aristotle. But in those days in Cambridge, the history of philosophy was sharply contrasted with doing philosophy proper. The former was devalued as essentially antiquarian: the latter was the real thing, to be practised in the style of the Wittgenstein of the *Philosophical Investigations*.

So one of the most shocking features of the divergence in European traditions of philosophy was the almost total silence, from those who taught philosophy at Cambridge, about Heidegger, about Nietzsche, even about Hegel. But it was not just a question of philosophy finding it difficult to travel northwards across the Channel, for it could be just as difficult going South. Philosophy faculties in France took almost as long to take seriously British or American

9

analytic philosophy in the style of A.J. Ayer or J.L. Austin or W.V.O. Quine as it did British – and some American – professors to pay adequate attention to much continental philosophy.

My opening remarks serve as a warning. Although in popular opinion, in many European countries especially, philosophy is supposed to be a clearly defined activity, a well-established discipline, part of what everyone should be familiar with if they are to count as decently educated, *which* philosophy is being talked about when such views are expressed is not at all clear. Who are the emblematic figures, Plato, Descartes, Kierkegaard, Marx, Husserl, Ryle, Derrida, who? There may be less confusion, at least there is explicit recognition of heterogeneity, when you have more than one philosophy department in the same university. That may be the outcome of bitter territorial disputes between different groups all appropriating the term 'philosophy' for their subject-matter or their way of studying it. But I was struck on my first visit to China, in 1987, by the peaceful coexistence, in the premier university in Beijing, Beijing daxue, Beida for short, of three separate departments, of Chinese Philosophy, Western Philosophy and Marxist Philosophy. But while there was coexistence, it also has to be said that there was not much communication between the three.

That leads inexorably to the question of whether, within what passes as Western philosophy, there is anything much in common between metaphysical system-building at one end of the spectrum and philosophical logic at the other. And where do ethics and politics, in theory or in practice, fit in? It used to be commonly argued that what held different branches of philosophy together was that they were all second-order investigations of some primary subject-matter, for example the analysis of what that subject-matter consisted in, or of the basis of its knowledge claims. Thus philosophy of science would be one example, philosophy of language another, philosophy of law a third. But to take all philosophy as 'philosophy of ...' is to assume what many would want to deny, namely that there is no primary subject-matter of philosophy itself.

But surely things were simpler in earlier times? There were certainly centuries in the European tradition when there was greater uniformity about what philosophy was supposed to do, namely meta-physics in the manner that stems from Plato and Aristotle and that, as theology, had often proved such powerful support for the Christian faith.[1] Yet that view, that philosophy is essentially a matter of the construction of a positive and systematic metaphysics, was secure only in the absence of, or in ignorance about, a countervailing scep-tical tradition, that would serve to undermine all such dogmatisms. As we recover more of the detail of later medieval and early modern philosophy, we can appreciate that the appearance of uniformity, at least in the goal of philosophy, is at points deceptive. Recent studies of the fortunes of the different brands of ancient Greek Scepticism (Burnyeat 1983, cf. Popkin 1979) have shown they often had a stronger presence than earlier standard histories assumed.

Of course Plato and Aristotle cannot be held responsible for what was done in their names. Nevertheless two points are clear and are fundamental to my theme. The first is that there was no uniformity about what 'philosophy' is or should be in Greek thought before Plato. The second, that Plato and Aristotle themselves began the reprocessing of earlier Greek thought in the light of their own – far from identical – images of philosophy (cf. most recently Frede 2004).

To test that, we have only to make the effort to recover some of the heterogeneity of what we conventionally call 'Presocratic philos-ophy', the thought of those individuals who appear in handbooks devoted to that subject, such as that of Kirk, Raven and Schofield (1983): Thales, Anaximander, Anaximenes, Pythagoras, Xenophanes, Heraclitus, Parmenides, Empedocles, Anaxagoras, Democritus and the rest. Some of these wrote in prose, others are poets, others just oral teachers; some are interested in moral issues as well as in nature and cosmology, others not; some in epistemology, others scarcely so, and so one can go on. Would they all have thought of themselves as engaged in the same single inquiry? As I have argued in detail else-where (Lloyd 2002b, but cf. Mansfeld 1990, Laks 2002), that seems extremely doubtful.

They certainly show no signs of all calling themselves 'philoso-phers'. The origins of the terms *philosophos* and *philosophia* are indeed unclear and disputed. Some ancient sources associate them with Pythagoras or the Pythagoreans (Diogenes Laertius I 12), but that can hardly be said to be certain. It is striking too that, in two of our earliest texts that use the term, it carries pejorative undertones. A fragment of Heraclitus (35) says that 'men who are *philosophoi* must be inquirers (*historas*) into many things indeed'. It is possible, but again not certain, that Heraclitus had Pythagoras, among others, in mind. In another fragment (129), the authenticity of which has however been doubted, Heraclitus says that 'Pythagoras son of Mnesarchus engaged in inquiry (*historiê*) most of all men' and it goes on to accuse him of a 'wisdom of his own', 'much learning' (*polumathiê*) and 'deceit'. It is clear, in any event, that Heraclitus had a negative view of inquiry, for his own recipe for finding wisdom was to 'search himself' (fr. 101). We may conclude that, whoever the *philosophoi* of fragment 35 were, Heraclitus did not approve of them. Pythagoras in person is quite definitely criticised when he is named with several others in another fragment (40) that exemplifies the dictum that 'much learning (*polumathiê* again) does not teach sense'. 'Otherwise', Heraclitus goes on, 'it would have taught Hesiod and Pythagoras, and again Xenophanes and Hecataeus.' It says a lot about the heterogeneity of the categories of learning that Pythagoras is here lumped together with the didactic poet Hesiod, the historian Hecataeus, and another poet, Xenophanes, who appears in collections of the 'Presocratic philosophers', but who was also famous for his compositions for symposia (male drinking parties).

The second text that shows how *philosophiê* could be no term of praise comes in the Hippocratic treatise *On Ancient Medicine*, of uncertain date but probably of the early fourth century BCE. In chapter 20 this writer criticises certain doctors and 'sophists' for holding that medicine depends on knowing about the elemental constitution of the body. But that, the writer says, takes you into '*philosophiê*', a word he evidently feels to be sufficiently unfamiliar that he needs to gloss it. He explains by referring to the kind of study that Empedocles engaged in and others who had written about nature (*peri phusios*), about the constitution of human beings and so on. But it is not that the Hippocratic writer approves of their endeavours. From the outset of the treatise he had been attacking those who based their medical theories and practices on arbitrary assumptions, *hupotheseis*, such as 'the hot', 'the cold', 'the wet', 'the dry' or 'anything else they fancy'. Medicine, he insists, is a *technê*, an art or skill, that must be based on long experience. Similarly in chapter 20 he criticises those who claim you need to study element theory first. On the contrary, he counters, if you want to find out about the human constitution, you have to do that from the study of medicine.

But would those we know as the Presocratic philosophers all have been happy to call themselves 'wise', *sophoi*? Yes and no. Certainly *sophos* can be a term of praise, as also can the term *mêtis*, 'cunning intelligence', associated especially with characters like Odysseus, the art of winning by fair means or even by foul provided you were not found out (Detienne and Vernant 1978). But *sophos* and *sophia* can also be used pejoratively, of those who are just cunning, or 'too clever by half'. More often they are used of skills that come some way between wisdom of the highest kind, on the one hand, and mere cunning, on the other, namely of expertise in an art or craft, and especially in poetry. But even if we could call all the 'philosophers' *sophoi* in *some* sense, that would not discriminate between them and many others – all those other poets, for instance. The Greeks had their Seven Wise Men (*sophoi*), though there was never complete agreement on who the Seven were. But they certainly included a variety of statesmen, such as Solon, Pittacus and Periander. Thales is the only one in the list who had some interest in the type of inquiry we associate with early Greek natural philosophy, and from our other evidence (e.g. Herodotus I 170) we know that he too won a reputation for the political advice he gave his fellow Ionians as well as for his business expertise: Aristotle (*Politics* 1259a5ff.) tells us that he predicted a bumper crop of olives, cornered the olive presses and made a fortune.

The one term that might be used to group together *most* of the entrants in the standard collections of 'Presocratic philosophers' is *peri phuseôs historia*, literally the inquiry concerning nature. Yet that too is problematic, for two main reasons. First, it was certainly not limited to those traditionally described (since Plato, say) as 'philosophers'. It would certainly have included some of those specu-

13

lative 'doctors and sophists' mentioned in *On Ancient Medicine*. Again, other Hippocratic writers would do perfectly well as practitioners – rather than as critics – of the inquiry into nature, such as the authors of *On the Nature of Man* (which engages in a detailed defence of pluralist element theory against versions of monism) and of *On Regimen* (which proposes an element theory based on fire and water and makes ample use of citations from Heraclitus, Empedocles, Anaxagoras, and others to help his argument along).

Secondly, and more importantly, the rubric of 'the inquiry into nature' will not do to cover the primary activities of two of the most influential Presocratic thinkers whom both Plato and Aristotle, in their different ways, acknowledge as their predecessors. One is Heraclitus, whose negative views about *historia* I have already mentioned. While he did not reject the evidence of the senses entirely (putting it in one fragment, 107, that 'eyes and ears are bad witnesses for men if they do not have souls that understand their language'), he was, on the interpretation I favour, committed to a highly counterintuitive view of change. Despite the appearances, that is despite the impression we have that many of the objects around us are quite stable, everything, Heraclitus claimed, without exception, is subject to constant change.

My second exception, Parmenides, took precisely the opposite view. Change is not only not constant: it is impossible. It is true that, after propounding a philosophy on the basis of the seemingly undeniable proposition that 'it is and it cannot not be', in the Way of Truth, Parmenides then went on, in the so-called Way of Seeming, to give an account of how things appear, a cosmology based on the two elements, Fire and Night. But if, in that section of his work, he engaged in an account of the natures of things 'so that no opinion of mortals shall outstrip you' (fr. 8.61) – in other words, in order to do better than any conventional cosmology – the validity of that whole exercise had already been totally undermined in the Way of Truth. Starting from it and the denial of what is not, we cannot justify any account of coming to be. As the later commentators put it, it does not come to be from what is (for that *is* already). Nor can it come to be from the totally non-existent. Moreover the denial of coming to be

14

leads to the denial of change (for that implies the coming to be of a new state of affairs, and *all* coming to be has been ruled out). Plurality too is rejected on the grounds that there is nothing that can separate what is from what is. I shall come back later to the implications of this style of philosophising, but for now need only note that it proves a major counter-example to those who might claim that the primary focus of interest of thinkers before Plato was the investigation into the natural world.

Parmenides' forte lay in the development of that rigorous deductive argument that I have just sketched so briefly, and in epistemology, where his rejection of the evidence of the senses was more radical than Heraclitus'. As fragment 7 puts it: 'do not let habit, born of experience, force you to let wander your heedless eye or echoing ear or tongue along this road, but judge by *logos* – reasoned argument – the much contested refutation spoken by me.' Others among the Presocratics show an interest in epistemology and methodology, several explore the relation between language and reality, many have critical views about the traditional gods and propose opinions of their own on their nature, and many too discuss soul or mind. But the trouble is that there is no one discipline, nor even a set of them, that all and only those who are conventionally grouped together as the Presocratic philosophers engage in. Every candidate study suffers from one or other or both of the two shortcomings that I have mentioned. Either there are generally recognised Presocratic philosophers who do *not* engage in it: or there are plenty of others, among the medical writers, for instance, who *also* show a developed interest in the study in question. The treatise *On the Art*, for example, talks about the relations between words and things, and *On Regimen* is one of several that put forward theories of the soul.

We are faced, then, with a double bind. To know what 'Presocratic philosophy' amounted to we have first to decide on who counts as a Presocratic philosopher. But to answer that question we have to have determined what Presocratic philosophy was. The problem is not just terminological. As we have seen, the word *philosophos* could be used with pejorative undertones: and it was sometimes applied very generally, not to an intellectual discipline so much as to intellectual

15

curiosity – as when Herodotus speaks of Solon 'philosophising' when he travelled the world to find out about things (I 30) or when Thucydides has Pericles say that the Athenians 'philosophise' without weakness when he has in mind such characteristics as their penchant for argument and rational explanation (II 40). The additional, substantial, factor that we have to take on board is that the intellectual interests of different individuals and groups in the period before Plato exhibit a coruscating variety.

None of the categories that we are used to applying, nor even those that the Greek themselves used at the time, is particularly stable. That point is generally acknowledged with regard to the term 'sophist', *sophistês*, about which I shall have something to say shortly. But it applies too even to such a category as that of doctor or healer, *iatros*. Styles of healing varied from the severely naturalistic to that practised in the shrines of healing gods or heroes, from the administration of drugs and surgical interventions, to cure by the word, by prayers, spells or incantations (Lloyd 2003). Not surprisingly, several of the writers who figure in the Hippocratic Corpus are concerned with the status of the medical *technê* and with the defence of medicine as an art or skill, rather than a matter of pure luck. I have noted the 'philosophical' interests of several of these authors, and to remind ourselves of the converse interests in medical matters on the part of philosophers we have only to think of Plato himself, who devotes a lengthy section of the *Timaeus* (81e-87b) to a theory of diseases, both those of the body and those that reach the soul through the body.

The fortunes of the term 'sophist' have a key role to play in our story. As is well known, both the noun *sophistês* and the verb *sophizesthai* are used non-pejoratively, indeed if anything with complimentary associations, in many early writers (Hesiod, Pindar, Herodotus, cf. Lloyd 1987: 91-8). But it came to be applied both by Aristophanes and by Plato especially, to an ill-defined assortment of teachers of whom they disapproved. Sometimes, as in Aristophanes (*Clouds*), the charge was that they corrupted the young by teaching how to make the 'worse' cause seem the 'better', though he was capable of making any clever new-fangled ideas the butt of his mockery. In Plato, the disapproval ranges from the mild (in the cases of such notable figures as Protagoras and Gorgias) to the extreme, where he uses the term generically for those who pervert the true cause of education – teaching virtue – for mercenary motives.

But while Aristophanes and Plato agree in their disapproval, that is almost all they agree on. Those criticised do not all teach the same range of subjects, though 'rhetoric' in one form or another is often implicated. We cannot, on the basis of our secondary sources, draw up an agreed, definitive, list of who counted as a 'sophist' or on what basis. Crucially, while Socrates is a stereotypical 'sophist' in Aristophanes, Plato used the category to drive a wedge between modes of intellectual activity he deplored and those he deemed representative of true 'philosophy', with Socrates himself, of course, a paradigm of the latter, not of the former. In the process it is not so much the image of the 'sophist' that is modified, as the model of the 'philosopher' himself.

Plato transformed both how the goal of the highest intellectual activity was to be defined, and the institutional framework within which it was to be pursued. Philosophy is now the disinterested search for truth, and the cultivation of virtue and the welfare of the soul, to be focused on single-mindedly, in the Socratic manner, with no thought for popularity or monetary reward.

Although the Academy that Plato founded owed something to earlier associations (Plato himself tells us, in *Republic* 600b, that Pythagoras taught his followers a way of life), this was the first recognisable Greek philosophical school. Yet it was certainly not just devoted to the search for truth and what we should call 'academic' studies, even if they were its primary concern. It was founded in part in the spirit of the dictum that kings should become philosophers or philosophers kings. The practical difficulties of implementing such a policy were borne in on Plato in the most dramatic fashion when his attempts to guide Dionysius II, ruler of Syracuse, in that direction ended disastrously, with Plato at one point imprisoned and in danger of his life. Yet Plato continued to be engaged in political theory throughout his career, following up the *Republic* with his second

17

massive political treatise, the *Laws*, on which he was still at work when he died. Moreover several of those associated with him in the Academy had distinct political ambitions, and not only the Syracusan adventurer Dion.[2]

While Plato's subsequent influence on the conception of 'philosophy' was immense, that certainly did not mean an end to philosophical pluralism. Rival views about what philosophy consists in appear already among Plato's own contemporaries. For Isocrates, for instance, the key was not Platonic dialectic, leading to the grasp of transcendental Forms, but the skills and wisdom the trained orator will exhibit in discussion, especially of practical affairs (Too 1995). While Aristotle agreed with Plato in rating the life devoted to philosophy as supreme, his ontology dictated a different conception of the goal. Explanation was still by way of forms, but they are instantiated by the phenomena to be explained, not (merely) imitated by them. It follows that close investigation of those phenomena is imperative.

The proliferation of the philosophical schools at Athens, first Aristotle's Lyceum, then the Hellenistic schools of Stoics, Epicureans, Cyrenaics, Cynics, Sceptics and others, did nothing to erode philosophical pluralism, but rather, on the contrary, institutionalised it. Each group offered its distinctive answers to the fundamental questions, and more than that, proposed divergent views as to what the fundamental questions were. Given that the schools were in competition with one another for pupils as well as prestige, the disagreements were often open and public, sometimes taking the form of formal debates. In those circumstances there was nothing to be gained from minimising the differences that separated you from your rivals: more often it was a case of maximising them. Philosophers regularly used their opponents the better to define and articulate their own positions.

That is particularly true of the Sceptics, who rejected 'dogmatic' views about underlying reality with the argument of *isostheneia*, 'equal strength'. For every such dogmatic view there was another of equal strength – but if of equal strength, then of equal weakness. So the Sceptics' recommendation was to suspend judgement. Yet while the dogmatists themselves evaluated the arguments on either side very differently, they often proceeded dialectically too, using the refutation of their opponents as a means of establishing their own position.

These Greek philosophical debates were one of the principal ways in which individuals or groups made their reputations, and they were one of the chief means whereby the schools attracted and held new members. We know that pupils 'shopped around', attending the lectures of more than one school, before deciding which to join, or indeed deciding to set one up for themselves.[3] Zeno of Citium, the founder of Stoicism, for instance, was taught first by Crates the Cynic, then by Stilpo the Megarian and by Polemo, who was head of Plato's Academy, before he went off to establish his own school at Athens. The third head of the Stoa, Chrysippus, was taught by the then head of the Academy, namely Arcesilaus, but then went on to criticise him. He was also taught by the second head of the Stoa, Cleanthes, not that he agreed with all of his views either. Yet when it came to who was to succeed Cleanthes, Chrysippus defeated his rival Ariston, even though Ariston had been taught by Zeno himself. Nor was it just in the Stoa that there were internal disagreements about the central tenets of the school and indeed the interpretation of what the founder himself stood for. In the Academy there was a notable dispute between Philo of Larissa and one of his ex-pupils, Antiochus, in the first century BCE, concerning the proper understanding of Plato himself.

In the circumstances I have described, the debates between and within the Greek philosophical schools were not just friendly gatherings of academics (in our sense) chatting about the latest technicalities in the subject. They were the battlefield on which the very survival of schools and the reputations of individuals were decided. Nor could you always necessarily trust those associated with you in the same school, for the possibility of defection was always there, even though in the case of the Epicureans, at least, that was rare. As I have argued elsewhere (Lloyd 1996a), both the philosophical and even the medical schools or sects, *haireseis*, should be thought of as more or less stable, more or less well-organised and

19

close-knit, alliances for defensive and offensive argumentative purposes, with the emphasis on that 'more or less'.

That situation was one stimulus, in my view, to the development of one distinctive feature of Greek philosophical inquiry, namely the interest, even the preoccupation, with second-order, that is epistemological and methodological, questions. Rather than just criticising your opponents for getting the solutions to the problems wrong, it was more effective to claim that they had misconstrued the nature of the problems in the first place. If you could show that their methods were incorrect, it would follow that their results were flawed. If you could argue that their understanding of the criteria of knowledge was imperfect, what they claimed to know was undermined. Meanwhile you could, and to some extent you needed to, argue positively for the truth of your own conclusions on the basis of the soundness of your own methodology. That helps to explain, I believe, that peculiarly Greek development of demonstration in the axiomatic-deductive mode, to which I shall be returning in other contexts. In a sense that was the ultimate argumentative weapon. Given self-evident primary premises and valid deductive reasoning, the conclusions were incontrovertible.

In the light of the pluralism I have thus sketched out, it is naturally difficult to offer a global characterisation of Greek 'philosophy'. But two general features stand out. First there is a contrast between those for whom philosophy is primarily and essentially a theoretical activity, aiming at truth, understanding and self-cultivation, on the one hand, and those, on the other, who emphasised its practical usefulness. Secondly, within those who focused on understanding, there was a further contrast in views as to how that was to be obtained. Let me elaborate both points to conclude this section.

For some, philosophy is an end in itself. For Aristotle it was the highest form of life, though he recognised that as citizens we need to practise the moral, as well as the intellectual, excellences. That philosophy was the key to securing happiness was a point on which the otherwise divergent Hellenistic schools agreed. Stoics, Epicureans, and even Sceptics all held that thanks to philosophy you could attain *ataraxia*, freedom from anxiety or other disturbance.

1. The Pluralism of Philosophical Traditions

That agreement is all the more striking in that the types of philosophising that led to that desirable outcome differed: for the dogmatic schools, you needed to be clear not just on ultimate physical reality, but also on what the good consisted in, virtue for the Stoics, pleasure for the Epicureans. But for the Sceptics it was not a positive doctrine on such subjects, but rather suspension of judgement, that gave you peace of mind: I shall have more to say on this in later chapters.

In the Hellenistic period (roughly, the last three centuries BCE), therefore, the view gained ground – among philosophers at least – that philosophy was essential for happiness. But it had always been held that aspects of it, at least, were of more direct practical utility. One reason for the popularity and success of many of those whom Plato labelled 'sophists' – but also for his distrust of them – was that they taught 'rhetoric', the art of persuasive speaking. Given the often intense involvement of many Greek citizens not just in the political processes of their city-states, but also in the law-courts, whether as litigants or as 'dicasts' (serving as both judge and jury, cf. Chapter 5), the abilities both to argue persuasively and to judge others' arguments were highly prized. While Aristotle shared some of Plato's reservations about the divorce of rhetorical skill from morality, he produced, nevertheless, his own technical analysis of what that skill consisted in, devoting three books indeed to teaching it.

Then the second important divergence of opinion divided those who agreed, at least, that the primary goal of philosophy was understanding. There were in fact two sharply contrasting views on the nature of the understanding to be sought. On the one hand there were those, like Parmenides, who insisted on following reason and abstract argument wherever they led. Their view was that philosophy should reconstruct how things had to be. If reasoned argument led to the conclusion that change and plurality are impossible, then the reaction was not to say that since change and plurality are obvious, something must have gone wrong with the argument, but rather to accept that change and plurality are illusory. No appeal to ordinary experience, or to the evidence of the senses, cut any ice with them, since they denied that the senses were veridical.

21

But against that view, Aristotle, for one, was a powerful spokesman for a fundamentally different conception of the task of philosophy, one in which the philosopher's job was not to argue *a priori* to how the world must be, but to explain how it actually is. That does not mean accepting, at face value, how the world appears to be. On the contrary, many common assumptions will, on examination, have to be radically revised – as, for example, the notion that the earth is flat. But the starting-point, and what has to be explained, is how things appear to be, and the aim of the exercise is to ascertain the causes that account for the phenomena we observe. Faced with those who denied change, Aristotle says that it is absurd to try to prove that it occurs, for there is no conceivable premise clearer than the conclusion from which that conclusion could be shown.

*

Let me turn now from ancient Greece to ancient China, where the problems of interpretation are, if anything, more severe. We have, to start with, a problem as to whether the terms 'philosophy' and 'philosopher' can be applied to classical China. The modern Chinese word for philosophy, *zhexue*, is an import from Japan in the nineteenth century, where those two Chinese graphs were used to represent European 'philosophy'. In ancient Chinese texts there is no such term: they speak rather, more generally, of learning, study, *xue*. Those who engaged in that aimed not just at developing cognitive skills, but at self-cultivation: and the goal of self-cultivation, spiritual, mental, physical, was, as Sivin has put it (Lloyd and Sivin 2002: 5) sagehood.

Then the second difficulty is analogous to the classificatory problems we encounter in ancient Greece, that of getting past the barriers presented by the traditional groups or schools into which Chinese thinkers are supposed to fall. The text-books speak of 'Confucians', 'Mohists', 'Daoists', 'Legalists', the School of Names (sometimes even labelled 'sophists') and so on, but in most cases we have to be very much on our guard. It is true that different accounts of various learned groups are presented in classical Chinese texts.

1. The Pluralism of Philosophical Traditions

One of the most influential is that proposed by Sima Tan in the final chapter of the *Shiji* ('Historical Records') (130), the work he began and his son Sima Qian completed around 90 BCE. But it has only recently begun to be appreciated how idiosyncratic that account was (Csikszentmihalyi and Nylan 2003). The key point is that he shifted attention from persons to convictions. His analysis itemises six intellectual tendencies, that were at the same time approaches to the *dao* (the Way) and to good government (we shall see the importance of that as time goes on). The only person he names is Mozi (Mo Di): otherwise the five comprise four abstractions (*yin-yang*, the law, names and the *dao* itself) together with the *ru*, a term which is almost invariably translated 'Confucian'.

Yet that term provides an excellent entry to the problems, for it certainly did not always imply some allegiance to the teachings of Confucius, even though it did in the case of Mencius in the late fourth century BCE and it may do so even in Sima Tan's view. Yet sometimes it suggested no more than conventional scholars regardless of affiliation (cf. Lloyd and Sivin 2002: 23) and it could be used pejoratively to imply snobbishness and pedantry. The problem with *yin-yang* and the *dao* (the tendency that Sima Tan himself favoured) is that those terms pick out ideas that are common ground to thinkers who used them in very different ways: I shall be coming back to that. As for the school of names, the label 'sophist' gets to be attached to the two chief representatives, namely Hui Shi in the fourth century BCE and Gongsun Long in the third, thanks to the interest both of them showed in paradox. Gongsun Long was famous for arguing that a white horse is not a horse. Yet this particular export of a Western category is quite misleading, in that their modes of operation were totally different from those of the individuals whom Plato and Aristophanes attacked. They certainly never gave public lectures to make their reputation and to attract fee-paying pupils.

The lessons we should learn from the problems of labels and classifications is that we have to get back to the individuals and the texts associated with them. Some of these are compilations or composite works, and in some cases their authenticity is open to question. Despite this, it is on the basis of those we can accept as genuine that we have to attempt the interpretation of Chinese thinkers at different periods – avoiding, as far as possible, the more misleading school affiliations that ancients and moderns have proposed.

Yet we can be sure that both pluralism and rivalry existed, especially, though certainly not exclusively, in the early Warring States period, before the unification of China under the Qin by Qin Shi Huang Di in 221 BCE. However, as we shall see, the rivalry especially takes a rather different form from its Greek manifestations. Although, as in Greece, this was sometimes a matter of competition for pupils, it was more often one of gaining the ear of the ruler.

I shall be considering alternative views of the *dao* in due course, but for now I note that it is common to criticise others for their inadequate grasp of it. It is not that these writers accuse their opponents of total ignorance (in the way that both Heraclitus and Parmenides dismiss the common run of humankind as deluded). Their criticism is more muted: their opponents have not comprehended *all* of the Way even though they may have had an inkling of some of it. Sima Tan makes such concessions in his account of other philosophical tendencies in the chapter of the *Shiji* mentioned above. Similarly the *Zhuangzi* text (which is a compilation of different strata from the fourth to the second century BCE) contains a chapter (*tianxia*, 33) that remarks of several figures that they had appreciated some, but not all, of the *dao*. The text names the legendary Lao Dan (the purported author of the *Dao De Jing*), Mo Di, a number of lesser figures, and even Zhuang Zhou (i.e. Zhuangzi, Master Zhuang) himself. They are all criticised at certain points, but all are said to have 'got wind of' some part of the ancient tradition of the *dao* and to have delighted in it.

More uncompromising attacks are also found. In the third century BCE the *Xunzi* devotes a chapter (6) to an attack on the 'Twelve Masters'. They included Mo Di, Hui Shi and both Zisi and Mencius, who shared with Xunzi himself some allegiance to Confucius. A little later in that century, the *Hanfeizi* (50) protests that the disagreements among the *ru* and among the Mohists were such that it was impossible in his day to be certain what either Confucius or Mo Di themselves taught.

Some of these disputes are less to do with doctrine than with behaviour. The *dao*, in any event, was not a matter of theory, but of approximating as closely as possible to the sage kings of old who had embodied it. The focus of many teachers was on the welfare of 'all under heaven' and on how that can be achieved. One striking feature of Chinese philosophy, when contrasted with Greek, is the large number of individuals who either held high office themselves or saw advising rulers as one of their chief roles. Confucius went from state to state and bemoaned the fact that he found no king worthy to receive his advice. Both Mencius and Xunzi are often represented as in audience with rulers. The Mohists set out to make themselves useful by becoming specialists in defensive warfare. Among those who acquired the label of the 'school of names', Hui Shi served as a minister and composed a law code for the king of Wei in the fourth century BCE, and Gongsun Long too is said to have been concerned, like everyone else, with order and good government. The 'Legalist' Han Fei was a nobleman and adviser to kings.

The pattern continues during and after the unification. One of the first great cosmological syntheses, the *Lüshi chunqiu*, was compiled under the auspices of Lü Buwei around 240 BCE. While he started as a merchant (so we are told in the *Shiji*), he became Prime Minister to the man who was to be the first Emperor. Around a century later, a second summa, the *Huainanzi*, was put together by Liu An who was prince of Huainan. The mastermind of what became the most influential Han cosmology, incorporating the notions of *yin-yang*, *qi* (breath/energy) and the five phases (often misinterpreted as Chinese element theory) was Dong Zhongshu, who had an admittedly chequered official career under the Han Emperor Wu Di.

Of course not all aspiring advisers were successful in obtaining positions of power and influence. Yang Xiong, responsible for an important cosmological poem, the *Tai Xuan Jing*, written at the turn of the millennium, never held an important office. A little later, in the first century CE, Wang Chong abandoned the only post he held, that of prefectural clerk, to write the *Lun Heng* in reclusion as a private teacher. In his case we may say that frustration at not holding office provided an important stimulus to original, critical, reflections on the beliefs and mores of his day.

25

Three aspects of this general ambition to advise those in positions of power deserve note. First, the interest in good government never stimulated, in China, reflections on the nature of the best political constitution. The universally accepted ideal was that of the benevolent rule of a wise monarch. The merits or demerits of other political arrangements, democratic, oligarchic or whatever, were never on the intellectual agenda, and there was never any question of experimenting with them in practice. The issues revolved round what that wise rule consisted in and how it could be ensured.

Secondly, involvement with those in authority often cost the advisers dear. The roll call of those who fell out with rulers and who came to a sticky end makes gruesome reading. Han Fei, Lü Buwei, Liu An all ended up being forced to commit suicide, and the historian Sima Qian would have done the same, but submitted to the ignominy of castration instead, out of filial piety towards his father, whose *Shiji* he felt he had an overriding obligation to complete.

That, thirdly, makes the dedication to the welfare of 'all under heaven' even more remarkable. It is true that some stood to gain more, some less, from good government if it could be achieved. But all agreed on the importance of that, and all shared the conviction that it implicated everyone in the kingdom or the Empire. The ideal was to that extent not a personal, egocentric one but one that affected all echelons of society.

Before I draw attention to some of the obvious similarities with and differences from ancient Greece, I must first consider how far this generalisation, about active interest and involvement in affairs of state, is valid for all the different strands of Chinese philosophical pluralism for which we have evidence. I have explained the difficulty of speaking of a group of 'Daoists', when the *dao* was common coin to most thinkers. But are not some of those who have been so labelled recluses who practised a policy of *wu wei* ('no ado', 'non intervention')? It is true that Zhuangzi is reported to have turned down a post as minister, preferring the life of a private individual,[4] though he is also said to have had, as his favourite debating partner, his friend Hui Shi, who held high office. But the *Zhuangzi* text uses the theme of *wu wei* in chapters that deal, precisely, with good government (for example, *Zhuangzi* 13). 'No ado' was a policy for private persons: but it was also adapted to apply to rulers. There the point was that the ruler should distance himself from the day-to-day business of government, delegating that to his ministers, and leading not by intervention but by example. Similarly, in another text often labelled Daoist, namely the *Huainanzi*, *wu wei* is recommended as a policy for governing (for example, *Huainanzi* IX 1a and 22b, XIV 9a). There were certainly Chinese recluses, at all periods, who turned their backs on politics. But the exceptions I have noted are just that and the general rule still stands.

Many of the comparisons and the contrasts with ancient Greece are obvious. Among the Presocratic philosophers, the Pythagoreans especially stand out for their reported involvement in politics. I mentioned Plato's disastrous Sicilian escapades and the relevance of the ambition to produce philosopher-kings to the programme of the Academy. Isocrates tried to influence Philip of Macedon and to have some impact on Greek policy vis-à-vis Persia, and there are quite a few Greek and Roman philosophers who were also statesmen at later periods. Seneca even shared Lü Buwei's fate, and Marcus Aurelius somehow combined Stoicism with imperial responsibilities.

But while the point certainly needs nuancing, there remains, in my view, an important contrast in what I might call the usual (and preferred) career patterns of Chinese and Greek philosophers. One way of making the point is by considering the role of philosophical schools and 'institutions of higher learning', though once again we have to be on our guard in relation to some of the Chinese evidence (Sivin 1995a). What modern scholars have called the 'Jixia Academy' in the kingdom of Qi in the fourth century BCE was in no sense a teaching institution, just an informal group of learned advisers. It followed the pattern of many courts of the Warring States period, where ambitious kings or ministers gathered round them 'guests' (*ke*) of different types. They could include entertainers and even hired assassins as well as advisers, though the Jixia group certainly contained more of the latter than most. There is of course a parallel with the situation that obtained in classical Greece, insofar as philosophers and 'sophists' could move from state to state and sometimes

27

frequented the courts of rulers. But as noted, the rivalry in Greece was for reputation among your peers, and for pupils, more than for patronage, of which less was available. Besides, in the democracies at least, there were no *permanent* rulers, like Chinese kings, for them to advise on government. Pericles, re-elected as general repeatedly from 443 until his death in 429, was very much the exception: and even he had to be re-elected every year (and was once deposed while in office) and carry the *dêmos* with him to implement his policies.

The contrast after the unification of China is more telling. The Chinese Imperial Academy was founded by the Han Emperor Wu Di in 124 BCE, who appointed a number of Erudites (*Boshi*) to teach official quotas of students. Already in 136 Wu Di had restricted state sponsorship to the teaching of the five Classics (the *Documents*, *Odes*, *Changes*, *Spring and Autumn Annals* and the *Rites*) and these formed the core curriculum of the Academy.[5]

On the one hand, the advantages to those who graduated from the Imperial Academy – as they did formally on passing their final examinations – were considerable. This was a recognised means of entry into the rapidly growing imperial civil service, and most students had that career in mind. We noted that Plato's Academy turned out some politicians, though that was not its primary purpose, nor that of the other philosophical schools at Athens. None provided those who attended them with a record of what they had achieved: none qualified them for an official career. When the Mediterranean world came under the domination of Rome, its eventual imperial civil service was staffed not by ex-students of the philosophical schools, but by freedmen and slaves.

On the other hand, the Chinese Imperial Academy had a monopoly of state-sponsored higher education, and though that did not mean an end to philosophical pluralism, it certainly restricted its growth. Where Greek philosophical reputations were generally made by impressing fellow-philosophers in the cut and thrust of the debates, both private and public, that always remained the prime activity of the philosophical schools, Chinese intellectuals continued to focus on the task of persuading the ruler of the value of their ideas, whether on government or any other matter. The standard format for the presentation of those ideas was the memorial to the throne. An apparent victory in abstract discussion counted for little compared with actually seeing your ideas put into practice by the person whose views really mattered. Indeed abstract discussion was not much cultivated, even though there was plenty of disagreement about the right policies to adopt to secure that wished-for welfare of all under heaven. Besides, apart from the satisfaction of getting something done in that regard, there was also the not unimportant payoff in terms of furthering your own career.

The point about abstract discussion can be illustrated by the differing fortunes of the interest in logic and language in China and in Greece. A series of Chinese writers, starting with Confucius himself, dealt with what was called the 'rectification of names', *zhengming*. This was, in practice, less a matter of the general use of language and the relation between words and things, than of ensuring that good order was maintained by the correct assignment of titles and social roles. Throughout the many subsequent discussions of the topic, the focus is on the importance of correct language use to avoid moral and political confusion.

I noted before that two philosophers from the so-called school of names, Hui Shi and Gongsun Long, explored paradox. In the writings of some of the later Mohists too there are discussions of ambiguity. But as they are presented, at least, these studies are not geared to logical questions (as we should call them) as such. The discussions of sameness and difference in meaning, of various types of paradox and modes of inference, formed part of a programme whose professed strategic aim was – as usual, one might say, in China – that of securing order and good government. That did not impress Xunzi, however. At the end of his chapter devoted to the rectification of names (22) he castigates such studies (admittedly without there naming Hui Shi and Gongsun Long personally) as deluded. These thinkers are mistaken in their use of words or in their understanding of realities, or in both, and they bring confusion both to names and to things. Xunzi's own verdict is clear. These are pernicious and inane theories, and the enlightened ruler will not argue with those who propound them.

Of course an interest in logic might have survived the criticisms of even such an influential figure as Xunzi, as well as the mockery of Zhuangzi, who deplored the wasted talents of Hui Shi. After all, such an interest developed in Greece even after the sophists had been attacked as immoral by Plato. But it could not have done so in China for the same reasons that applied in Greece, where logic was seen as an important tool for philosophy, in that it provided the means to justify the validity of your arguments and even to demonstrate your conclusions, and where it was linked to those second-order interests in methodology and epistemology that I have mentioned.[6] It is significant that in China the one area of argumentation that did receive sustained and sophisticated discussion (in *Hanfeizi* 12, for instance) was not the formal analysis of validity, but the psychology of persuasion – crucial, to be sure, if you were to succeed in gaining the ear of the ruler, to win him round and at the same time not be seen to be manipulating him.

The categories of intellectual we find in China are as varied as those in Greece. In addition to the 'itinerant advisers' (*youshui*) and the erudites (*boshi*), there are those named after the specific studies they engaged in, doctors, mathematicians (specialists in *shu shu*)[7] astronomers (experts in *tianwen* and *lifa*)[8] and many others, the boundaries of which and between which are sometimes as hard to delineate as those separating their Greek approximate counterparts. Those responsible for the syntheses I have mentioned, the *Lüshi chunqiu* and the *Huainanzi*, incorporated ideas not just from different philosophical groups, but also from technical specialists. Conversely, the medical classic, the *Huangdi neijing*, put together around the turn of the millennium, deals with the microcosm of the body in terms that draw on the wider principles, of *yin-yang* and the five phases, that apply to the macrocosm and to the state. What counts as 'philosophy' in China, like its counterpart in Greece, is not a single discipline so much as a series of interrelated studies with ramifications in most areas of intellectual activity.

*

1. The Pluralism of Philosophical Traditions

Two questions need now to be faced in conclusion. First, how far is it possible to arrive at valid general characterisations of the differing pluralisms that we find in the philosophical traditions of ancient Greece and China? Second, what can we glean from this that is relevant to the conception and practice of philosophy today?

What were philosophy, the love of wisdom, or learning, or understanding, or even knowledge, good for in ancient China or Greece? The answers in both cases are complex. Some ambitions were decidedly practical in orientation, to produce good order or secure other improvements in the public domain. Others are more theoretical: to understand, rather than to change things – to grasp their causes, for instance. Others again are more inward-looking, private, even idiosyncratic, the pursuit of individual self-fulfilment or self-cultivation, no mere matter of the exercise of intellectual capacities. Many individuals, more mundanely, undertook the studies they did simply to gain a reputation for cleverness and to make a living, whether by teaching, or by acquiring the support of a patron, or by qualifying themselves for appointment to an office. I shall be returning in my final chapter to the issue of the diversity of values and ideals in play.

But while the range of possible ambitions covers a similar spectrum in both China and Greece, where the emphasis falls within that spectrum does differ – at least if we are to judge by the impressions created by extant writers concerning how they saw who made the running. While not all Chinese advisers focused exclusively on the social, moral and political problems that centre round good government, there is an important consensus on its strategic importance, even while the variety of ideas on how to achieve it was considerable, ranging from the advocacy of inaction and leading by example, to the insistence on the tightest measures of social control. But the effect of that concentration or focus was to allow only limited scope for more abstract or theoretical inquiries in such areas as the investigation of logic and language.

The history of Greek philosophy, by contrast, is one where abstract speculation was often given full rein. We saw that some extravagantly counter-intuitive ideas were entertained, such as the denial of change. Some were convinced that the job of the philosopher is to

31

deduce, by rational argument, what *must* be the case, rather than to explain, by whatever means possible, how it is. Yet while, compared with Chinese traditions, there was an exceptionally heavy concentration, in ancient Greece, on epistemological and methodological issues, there was also a strong sense, running through otherwise divergent schools of thought, that philosophy is no mere academic study, but the key to how we should live, to happiness or well-being.

Then there is this further difference in emphasis, between what were generally the dominant conceptions in China and in Greece, that the Greeks tended to see happiness as a personal or individual matter, possible though difficult even in an unjust state. The Chinese focus on good government was a focus on what could or should in principle serve to benefit 'all under heaven', even though there was never any doubt that different individuals would have markedly different roles within the social order.

What then does this rapid survey of ancient Greek and Chinese philosophical pluralisms suggest for us today? The history of philosophy should be a resource for philosophising. That does not mean that it should lead us to propose some new general prescription for philosophical correctness, some post-post-modernism, some post-anti-logocentrism, or any other -ism. We are concerned to try to attain critical understanding of such important fields as morality and science: I use both terms to span both practice and theory. The goal, in the former case, is surely the one that Socrates pointed to – not just to try to understand what it is to be good, but indeed to be good. The philosopher of science, similarly, has a particular task of investigating what it is to understand physics or cosmology or genetics: but that cannot be divorced from understanding them.

The history of philosophy shows that there can be different balances, between theory and practice, different orientations as between being and doing, and explaining and understanding. It reveals, too, the different effects of the different institutional frameworks (in the broadest sense) in which philosophical inquiry was undertaken. We are invariably involved, as historians, in evaluation, since no description can be totally value-free. That carries with it the particular obligation to be self-aware and self-critical. There is no

Olympian vantage-point from which definitive assessments can be made. All must be subject to revision: all must come to the pragmatic test of whether they withstand critical scrutiny, whether in that sense they work.

Certain of the excesses to which both some Greek and some Chinese traditions were prone are easily recognisable. The Greek demand for ultimate foundations has indeed been heavily criticised in recent decades. The opposite extreme to which the insistence on the ineffability of the truth is liable is that that can sometimes seem to be an excuse – where we need to probe the nature of the claim and its grounds and where it seems too easy to be content with the observation that ultimate understanding is unattainable. But both the proponents of *logos* and those of the *dao* would have agreed, from their different perspectives, that exercising judgement, let alone living up to the highest ideals that they set, is no easy matter.

If from our perspective we can diagnose what I have called their excesses, that does not mean, of course, that we are necessarily any better at diagnosing our own. In particular we may not be any better at recognising the effects of the institutional framework within which we operate, of the professional deformation we may suffer, and of the influences of the different types of situation of communicative exchange in which we engage.

One lesson that a study of ancient endeavours serves to bring out is that to treat philosophy as an academic study in our sense, that is primarily as an intellectual exercise, is to neglect or ignore what many, indeed most ancient Chinese and Greeks undertook those endeavours for. There is a striking contrast between, on the one hand, the modern academic sceptic, whose scepticism is a solution to certain abstract problems that has no impact on his or her career decisions or conduct of life, and, on the other, the ancient Greek Sceptics, or Cynics, or Stoics, who attracted the amazement and the admiration, if also the criticism, of their own contemporaries because they lived by the philosophical views they held. Then, outside the Academy, we have lost the Chinese insight that a primary, if uncomfortable, responsibility is to remonstrate, where necessary, with those who rule us and to advise on good government – not that we should agree with the ancient Chinese on what that consisted in nor on how it should be implemented.

No doubt qualifications need to be entered and some exceptions granted. It is certainly better that any philosophy that savours of authoritarianism or of dogmatism – such as many metaphysical systems of the past have done and some still do – should be confined to merely academic study rather than be taken as guidance for life. Admiring Plato's *Republic* as political analysis should not be confused with wanting to put his policies into practice. As for exceptions, even modern philosophers become members of Think Tanks and produce influential policy documents: others may be called in on specific moral issues, such as abortion or drugs, when government recognises the need to legislate: yet others, though rarely in most countries, may get to hold ministerial positions. The occasional outspoken critic of government policies achieves some notoriety – though where Chomsky, for one, is concerned, there is often little sense of the connection between his political stance and his technical philosophical studies. But those exceptions do not alter the general perception much. In the UK, as well as in the USA, politicians, and the public as a whole, commonly assume that philosophers have no business outside their ivory towers, and in America especially that often goes with the view that they had better behave themselves in them, if they are not to incur the wrath of the authorities for dissident, un-American, activities.

But if philosophers often feel sidelined, we have only ourselves to blame – for the way we define the subject as an academic one, and encourage our pupils to do the same, and for the manner in which we fight shy of alternative views of what it may be good for. Insofar as that is correct, a first step to improve the situation is surely to use the history of philosophy, and the study of ancient Greece and China in particular, to help unmask our own philosophical parochialisms – the point from which I began my investigation in this chapter.

2

Learned Elites: their Training,
Openness and Control

My first chapter explored a number of aspects of the philosophical pluralisms of ancient Greece and China, which I examined largely from the point of view of the variety of models, styles and aims that can be exemplified. An important set of related questions that now needs separate elaboration concerns the constitution of learned elites, the qualifications or training that were required or expected, how access to them was gained, and how (if indeed at all) they were controlled and by whom. We may broaden the scope of our inquiry in two ways, first by including, and indeed focusing especially on, technical specialists such as doctors, mathematicians and astronomers, and secondly by taking advantage of the rich evidence on these questions that comes from a third ancient civilisation, namely Mesopotamia.[1]

The chief questions we need to consider are the following. What, first, were the titles or roles or offices that marked out more, or less, prestigious membership of the elite? How well delineated were they? Who had, or could claim, a right to them, or how was access to them obtained? Was that by virtue of birth or family? Did you get the job because your father had had it before you? Or because you were wealthy? Did you rely on influential patrons? Did you have to serve an apprenticeship and did that involve initiation, oath-taking or other commitment to loyalty? What other instruction did you receive and was your competence tested by examination? To what extent could an individual bypass all formal procedures and get on with the job on their own, tackling problems that others could not handle, if they were a mathematician for instance, or proving successful in medical practice, however 'success' was judged? How far, in other words, were the elites open to just anyone with enough talent and

35

ambition to break in? How permeable were the boundaries circumscribing the elites? With what kinds of institutional or intellectual barriers were they defended and how effective were those defences?

My strategic aims are first to see what a review of such issues can tell us about the organisation, internal structure and openness of learned elites in the three ancient civilisations I have targeted, and then to consider what reflections they suggest concerning our own, on the face of it, very different situation. The stages of instruction that a budding scientist now has to pass through - undergraduate degree, PhD, post-doctoral positions - present a formidable array of rites of passage. How well are the modes of openness we want served by the systems we have in place? An examination of earlier times may have lessons for us even today, at least in that it may make us think hard – or harder – about the relations between the scientific work done in any society and that society's favoured institutions and values.

I have posed the questions using a number of obviously anachronistic categories. The terms 'astronomer', 'mathematician', 'doctor' even, are all potentially misleading, begging a lot of questions regarding how the people concerned saw themselves and their work. That applies even more particularly to 'scientist', for, as is well known, nobody spoke of 'scientists' as such until that term was coined by Whewell in the nineteenth century. But provided we are prepared to rethink our categories, revise our assumptions, and think ourselves back to a very different world with what may seem to us strange institutions and practices, we can, I believe, make a first stab at the answers to the questions I began with.

The Mesopotamians, Chinese and Greeks were all concerned to get the calendar right, to determine and predict the movements of the heavenly bodies, to treat the sick. The variety of ways in which they conceived those activities, and the different types of learned cadres that were put in charge, pose interesting and difficult questions for our inquiry. Global solutions or answers are out of the question. Indeed we should not attempt to generalise about 'Mesopotamia' as a whole, or about 'China' or about 'Greece'. But if we are careful to differentiate within fields and between periods, we can make some tentative suggestions concerning some aspects of the problems for *some* of the groups we can identify at *some* periods. In particular there appear to be interesting connections between the structure of some of the groups in question and the intellectual practices – especially the argumentative tactics – they engaged in, which is an issue I shall take up again in Chapter 3.

*

We may begin with Mesopotamia, where the Letters and Reports from Assyrian and Babylonian scholars that mostly date from the eighth and seventh centuries BCE are our most important source. The titles of the key posts and positions are clear – not that the jobs that went with the titles remained unchanged throughout the fluctuations in Mesopotamian history. First there are general terms that denote the learned or the wise as a whole. Thus *ummânu* and *ummânu mudû* are used of Master-scholars in general. Then, most important for our purposes, are the titles that correspond to specific, more or less professional, functions. I shall be reviewing those shortly. In addition, thirdly, we have considerable lists of officials in the palaces and at court. They name a wide variety of posts - military, administrative and domestic - ranging from 'governor' and 'cohort commander of the crown prince' and 'horse trainer of the open chariotry' all the way to 'cup-bearers', 'cooks', 'tailors' and 'butchers' (Fales and Postgate 1992: tablets 3-5 and 21, pp. 6ff., 28). Most of the posts in those general lists do not relate to scholarly activities and so fall outside our discussion here. But there are exceptions, namely references to certain 'scribes' and 'lamentation singers', and in some of the more specific lists the categories mentioned relate to experts of one kind or another (e.g. Fales and Postgate 1992: tablet 1, pp 4ff).

Thus Parpola (1993: xiii ff.) has identified five specific scholarly disciplines that are of particular importance. These are (with his translations), *tupšarru* (astrologer/scribe), *bārû* (haruspex/diviner), *āšipu* (exorcist/magician), *asû* (physician) and *kalû* (lamentation chanter). These renderings have to be taken with a pinch of salt. Exorcist/magician for *āšipu*, for instance, does not capture the fact that they, as well as the *asû*, often dealt with the sick, and it is very doubtful whether the category of 'magic' is at all appropriate. In addition we hear of *šā'ilu* (dream interpreters) and individuals who are given the title *ērib bīti* ('enterer of the temple'). Among the *ṭupšarru*, some are identified as *ṭupšarru Enūma Anu Enlil*: these are the scribes that dealt with the celestial omen series, *Enūma Anu Enlil*, the vast compendium of lore concerning the heavens that was put together between 1500 and 1200 BCE but contains much even earlier material. They have been the subject of recent studies by Rochberg (2000, 2004) that bring out certain fundamental points (cf. Oppenheim 1969, Brown 2000: ch. 1).

First, those who write commentaries on the *Enūma Anu Enlil* are not always given that title.

Secondly and conversely, those who have the title are not concerned exclusively with *Enūma Anu Enlil*, since they deal with other canonical divinatory texts as well, for example *Šumma izbu* (the so-called anomaly series) and *Šumma ālu* (the terrestrial omen series) (Rochberg 2000: 360-1, Oppenheim 1969: 99). Divination figures throughout: but it should be borne in mind that that generally involved close observation of the empirical phenomena, the signs, themselves.

Thirdly, the five specific functions in Parpola's list are not mutually exclusive. Some individuals have more than one competence. Rochberg 2000: 366 cites the case of one scribe from Uruk, named Iqīšâ, who was an *āšipu*, who owned a number of astronomical-astrological texts and who was also called *ērib bīti Anu u Antu*, that is 'enterer of the temple of Anu and Antu'. The scribe Marduk-šāpik-zēri, the author of one letter to Assurbanipal (Parpola 1993: tablet 160, pp. 120ff.), is a positive polymath. He says he follows his father's profession of *kalû*: as a 'lamentation singer' he was responsible for certain apotropaic rituals, among other things. However, he also claims knowledge of purificatory rituals and of disease. He has studied *Enūma Anu Enlil*: he has made observations of the heavens, and he has also read the *Šumma izbu*, the *Šumma ālu* and works dealing with physiognomy (Parpola 1993: tablet 160, p. 122, Rochberg 2000: 361). Whether or to what extent any scholar –

ummânu – was expected or obliged to be learned in the entire range of canonical texts is, however, unclear.[2]

Fourthly, many, but not all, scribes come from families whose members had held similar functions. This was the case with Marduk-šāpik-zēri, as we have just noted, and Brown 2000, 36ff., is able to trace the family ties of several groups of Assyrian and Babylonian scholars working on astronomical-astrological matters. Birth evidently counted for a good deal among the circles of the learned elite, although it would be to go beyond the evidence to suggest that skills were *always* handed down from father to son.

It is clear, fifthly, that some of the knowledge these professionals mastered is esoteric. Several of the texts refer to the 'secrets of heaven and earth' or to the 'secrets of the great gods' (Rochberg 2000: 363-2, cf. Lambert 1967). There are some occasions when a text is described as having been revealed by a god, for example in a dream, to a particular scribe. But several canonical series are ascribed more generally to a god. Thus *Enūma Anu Enlil*, the corpus of the *āšipu*, and that of the *kalû*, are all three ascribed to the god Ea. Other tablets speak of the divination texts as the 'secrets of Anu, Enlil and Ea', or as knowledge revealed first to the sage Enmeduranki and then to the 'men of Nippur, Siddar and Babylon' (Rochberg 2000: 363, Lambert 1967: 132).

This takes us, sixthly, to other qualifications that were expected of those who entered the ranks of these elite professions. Rochberg 2000: 363, comments on the text just mentioned that 'the diviner must be without physical blemish, must be considered a descendant of Enmeduranki the sage … and must be sworn by an oath "on tablet and stylus before Šamaš and Adad" before being instructed … in the discipline by an *ummânu*.' However, we know from other evidence that there were exceptions to that rule about physical purity, at least for some callings. Marduk-šāpik-zēri recommends twenty of his pupils or apprentices for employment by the king, among whom are certain refugees from Assyria. One of these, named Aqrea, is said to have been branded on the face and wrists, but to be, nevertheless, a capable *āšipu*. Sometimes, it seems, scholarly expertise counted for more than freedom from physical taint or other civil disadvantage.

It is clear, moreover, seventhly, that competence was not just a matter of mastery of a text, but also of knowing what to do. These scholars had to be experts in carrying out certain rituals. One important procedure was that of *namburbû*, the substitution of a criminal for the king, so that any misfortune that had been predicted fell on the one and not on the other. Scholars were evidently graded in a hierarchy of ranks, from mere apprentices, through (ordinary) scholar, to Master (Brown 2000: 48ff.). A chief scribe, for instance, was known as *rab ṭupšarri*.

Two important points need to be added in conclusion. First, we must recognise that the roles of the *ṭupšarru Enuma Anu Enlil* and of other members of the literate elite were far from static over the many centuries during which we hear of their operations. In particular, the main base of the *ṭupšarru* shifted from the palaces or courts of kings, to the temples. Some neo-Assyrian *kalûs* and possibly also *āšipus* were consecrated members of temples, though they did not have the title 'priest' (šangû) (Rochberg 2000: 369). Moreover, while the vast majority of the scholars were officials of one type or another, Brinkman 1990 has pointed out that, in the case of some of those who were responsible for Babylonian chronicles, there is no direct evidence of an attachment to the court, and it is possible that some of these were private, or at least non-official, individuals.

Secondly, although we have noted the relevance of some non-technical qualifications, it is clear that the Mesopotamian scribes were evaluated, overwhelmingly, by their mastery of the canonical texts. That may suggest that they must have been ultra-conservative, but again caution is needed. From the eighth century onwards, as Brown 2000 has shown, the scribes became increasingly confident in their ability to predict a variety of celestial phenomena. There is a shift in the form of some at least of their predictions. They no longer take the form of conditionals in which the protasis refers to a celestial event and the apodosis gives its interpretation: if so and so, then that means such and such good or bad fortune for the king or his enemies. They come to relate to the celestial events themselves, where the predictions concern such matters as the first or last visibility of planets, the possibility or impossibility of both lunar and solar eclipses and even, in some tablets, their occurrence.

2. Learned Elites: their Training, Openness and Control

Yet that increasing confidence did not mean that less attention was paid to *Enūma Anu Enlil*. On the contrary, interpretations of what was observed still generally proceeded by reference to what that text had laid down, and this poses a problem. Even though the scribes knew perfectly well – so it would appear – that eclipses can take place only at the new or full moon, they still sometimes concern themselves with the hypothetical possibility of occurrences on what we would consider impossible days. How to interpret this is a subject of considerable dispute. One view has it that it was simply the prestige of *Enūma Anu Enlil* itself, and the fact that it entertained the possibility of such occurrences, that dictated that the scribes should continue to list them. Another is that some of them did not rule out the suspension of what they nevertheless knew to be the normal regularities: one tablet says that the gods can do anything, though without specifying everything that covers.

To summarise the situation in our first civilisation: we already find a well-organised and quite highly differentiated literate elite. Mastery of the canonical texts was not the sole qualification needed for entry, but it was by far the most important.

*

Many of the same or similar features emerge from the evidence for learned elites in ancient China. Here too we can distinguish between generic titles and more specific ones, and here too there are notable shifts in the meaning and reference of key terms. We have already encountered, in the last chapter, two of the general terms, *ru* and *boshi*, and a third, the most general of all, *shi*, forms the second element in that last expression.

Ru, as I pointed out, is often translated 'Confucian', but that is an oversimplification. In the Han period, the term was used 'sometimes for members of a lineage that claimed descent from Confucius, but more often for conventional scholars regardless of affiliation' (Sivin in Lloyd and Sivin 2002: 23). Later the word came to be used by writers looking for precursors for a class of teachers who tutored descendants of noble families in manners, morals or other basic attainments or skills. However, as I also noted before, it can be used negatively, with pejorative undertones of snobbishness and pedantry.

The second term, *boshi* ('scholars of broad learning') came to be the most usual title for the 'erudites' associated with the Imperial Academy – where that role is sometimes translated, in English, as 'Academician'. But originally it had been a label for learned ritual and political consultants more generally. The second element in the expression, *shi*, underwent shifts that Sivin has charted, comparing them indeed with the transformations in the English word 'gentleman' (Sivin in Lloyd and Sivin 2002: 16ff.). In the eighth century BCE, *shi* referred to the lower strata of hereditary aristocrats entitled to bear arms, but it came to be used of 'all sorts of wellborn men, no longer bred to fight, no longer heirs to power, supporting themselves by official employment, patronage and other pursuits that required literacy or other expertise'. By 100 BCE they were likely to be 'landowners, wellborn but seldom titled, and usually literate', but by 200 CE *shi* 'tended to come from wealthy families (now wellborn by definition) and to be educated in the classics'. There is, then, an interesting shift in the balance of the mixture of birth, wealth and learning, that the title implied at different times.

But if at one end of the spectrum, there are various appellations for members of the literate elite in general, at the other end, in China as in Mesopotamia, there are specific titles for officials and functionaries of different types. Already in Han times, there is a vast proliferation of these, ranging from the three great offices of State, 'Chancellor' (*chengxiang*), 'Imperial Counsellor' (*yushi dafu*) and 'Supreme Commander' (*tai wei*), through the nine Ministers (*jiu qing*), all the way to the mass of junior posts in the various departments of the increasingly elaborate and complex bureaucracy on which the running of the Empire depended.

The dynastic histories are a mine of information on these. The *History of the Later Han (Hou Hanshu)*, in particular, devoted five whole treatises, 24-28, to the officials of state, specifying their duties, reporting their pay, giving the titles and numbers of the subordinates assigned to the higher officials and much else besides. There were some seventeen or eighteen different ranks of officials, ranging from those with annual pay of 10,000 bushels (of grain) to those on 100 bushels or less. The senior 'Grand Imperial Physician' (*taiyi ling*) was on 1000 bushels and his chief assistant was on 600, as also, however, was the 'Grand Sacrificial Butcher' (*taizai ling*). In the Astronomical Bureau, charged with the two main divisions of the study of the heavens, namely *tianwen* and *lifa*, there were, at the top of the hierarchy, officials who reported direct to the Emperor and advised him on what the heavens had to say about how his mandate stood. But in the lower echelons, there were numbers of 'expectant officials' (*daizhao*), 'observers' (*wanglang*) and 'clerks' (*zhanggu*), responsible for the humdrum business of carrying out and recording the necessary observations. Again, as in Mesopotamia, the titles and functions did not remain static. Bielenstein 1980 sets out the situation in Han times, and Hucker 1985 charts the changes that occurred from the earliest dynasties all the way down to the Qing.

We have concrete evidence concerning the training and qualifications of some of those who held the interestingly complex post of *taishi* or *taishi ling*. English translations of this vary confusingly between Grand Scribe, Grand Historian or Grand Historiographer, to Grand Astrologer or even Astronomer Royal (cf. Lloyd 2002a: 9). When we encounter individuals with that title or, what is the equivalent, *dashi*, in the *Shiji* or the *Zuozhuan*,[3] we find them undertaking a variety of roles. These certainly include acting as a recorder of events, i.e. scribe or historian in that sense. But they are also consulted on ritual matters (in the *Lüshi chunqiu* the *taishi* announces important dates in the calendar), and they carry out divinations or interpret those conducted by others and omens and prodigies generally. The great historians Sima Tan and his son Sima Qian (responsible for the *Shiji* compiled around 90 BCE) both held that position – at least until Sima Qian's disgrace when he fell from favour with the Emperor Wu Di for daring to imply some criticisms of his policy with regard to the Xiong Nu, the Huns.

Sima Tan further reports his own early training in *Shiji* 130. From this it is clear that he received a general education that included instruction in the *dao* and in the great divination and cosmological classic, the *Yijing* or *Book of Changes*, as well as in the study of the heavens. A *taishi* certainly needed to be proficient in calendrical matters, though he would not necessarily be involved in calendar reform, and as a diviner he might be called upon to interpret signs from heaven. In the *Hou Hanshu* treatise 25: 3572, the duties of the *taishi ling* are specified as (1) being in charge of the calendar and ephemerides (tables of celestial movements), (2) choosing auspicious dates and times for state business, sacrifices, funerals, weddings and so on, and (3) recording propitious and unpropitious omens as they occurred.

From the end of the second century BCE, the 'higher education' of all members of the Chinese literate elite was centred on the institution I discussed briefly in Chapter 1. The Imperial, or Grand, Academy (*tai xue*), founded by the Emperor Wu Di, started modestly, with a quota of fifty enrolled students in 124 BCE. But by the second century CE the figure had grown to the admittedly round number of '30,000'. Already in 136 BCE, as I noted, the five classics gained official recognition to the exclusion of the writings of other masters, and they came to form the core curriculum of the Academy.

Entry came to be by written examination and indeed there were further examinations on graduation. That certainly allowed merit to be rewarded: advancement did not just depend on birth, or patronage, or wealth. Talented individuals from outside noble families could succeed and rise to positions of power and authority in the state. But the point should not be exaggerated. The qualifications of entrants, as these were set out in the founding document of the Academy, put the emphasis on respectability. They were to be 'those of seventeen years or older, of serious manner and deportment ..., fond of cultivation through study, respectful towards elders and superiors, with a respectful attitude towards the government's enactments and its moral teachings' (I cite Sivin's translation of *Hanshu* [*History of the Han*] 88: 3594 in Lloyd and Sivin 2002, 50).

In general, then, those who sought a career in the Chinese civil service (and that was indeed the normal ambition of members of the literate elite) had to be educated in the classics. But technical training was also available in 'astronomy', 'mathematics' and 'medicine'.

44

2. Learned Elites: their Training, Openness and Control

Already around the turn of the millennium, two technical treatises existed in the first two of those fields. The *Zhoubi suanjing* ('*Arithmetic Classic of the Zhou Gnomon*') dealt mainly with astronomical problems. The *Jiuzhang suanshu* (*Nine Chapters on Mathematical Procedures*) provided an analysis of sets of mathematical problems that was more comprehensive than the earlier, simpler, second-century BCE compendium, the *Suanshushu* (Book of Arithmetic). These works throw light both on what was taught, and on how.

In the *Zhoubi suanjing* ch. 1, the teacher, Chenzi, takes the pupil, named Rong Fang, through a series of problems, including how to calculate the height of the sun and the distance to the sub-solar point on the assumption of a flat earth. But he does not explain his procedures until Rong Fang confesses his own inability to work them out for himself. Similarly in the *Nine Chapters*, the sections called the Method give the solutions to the problems set out, but it is largely left to the commentators, starting with Liu Hui in the third century CE, to explain how these are obtained. In these cases, as often elsewhere in the learned disciplines in China, we may suppose that the written text was to be supplemented by oral instruction by a master. A great deal, however, was evidently left to the pupil to work out on his own. As Confucius is supposed to have held (*Lunyu* 7.8), if a pupil, on being shown one corner, was unable to infer the other three for himself, then he was not worth teaching.

The situation in Chinese medicine and medical education bears certain generic similarities to what we have found in astronomy and mathematics, though there are certainly differences in emphasis. We have seen from Sima Tan and his son that some offices ran in families: Sima Tan claims, at least, that his family had been *taishi* for generations. But birth may have been particularly important in medicine. As Sivin has put it (Lloyd and Sivin 2002: 23), 'the great majority of therapists inherited their occupations and were unable to read and write'.

Elite physicians, however, were likely to be literate and some were positively learned. We have detailed evidence concerning the training of one mid-second-century BCE doctor called Chunyu Yi in the biography devoted to him in the *Shiji* (105). From this it becomes clear first that he was taught by more than one physician, though he did not just pick and choose who to go to (in the manner of some Greeks). He moved from the first to the second on the recommendation of the former. Secondly, he was not related by birth to either teacher, although one of them indicates that it would normally be expected that he would train members of his own family. Chunyu Yi is warned not to reveal to the members of his teacher's family that he has received instruction. Thirdly, both teachers hand on texts as well as teaching to him. Moreover, fourthly, some of that learning is esoteric and was not to be divulged to others. His first main teacher, Gongsun Guang, instructs him not to teach his formularies to anyone else, and his second, Gongsheng Yangqing, also describes his formularies as 'secret'. Finally, before Yangqing accepts him, Chunyu Yi serves him and it is only after a period of evaluation that Yangqing finally decides to take him on as a disciple. When at last he is accepted, Chunyu Yi expresses how fortunate he is and marks his new status by making obeisance to his master.

Elsewhere too in our sources we have further evidence of the rites of passage that could be involved in joining the ranks of elite physicians. Sivin 1995b, 184f., has discussed the account in the *Huangdi neijing lingshu* 48,1: 396, where the Yellow Emperor (here represented as the teacher) accepts the Thunder Duke (Lei Gong) as pupil. He is told that he has to take the oath.[4] After purifying himself for three days, he seeks permission and the oath is then sealed by cutting the arm and smearing the blood. The Yellow Emperor recites: 'Today at the epochal time of *yang* we smear the blood, transmit the formulas. He who dares defy these words will surely suffer.' The Thunder Duke bows repeatedly and the Yellow Emperor takes him by the left hand, and with his right, hands him the book, saying: 'Take care, take care. I will now explain it to you.'

Thus we see that in certain contexts in medicine family ties were important, rites of initiation were compulsory and access to the texts that contained the lore privileged. Yet the evidence also suggests that the relative importance of those factors varied, and in particular the kinship between master and pupil was sometimes symbolic rather than actual. That was also the case sometimes in the broader field of philosophical learning. There the term that eventually came to be used of philosophical lineages, namely *jia*, literally 'families', underwent considerable shifts in sense and reference, as Csikszentmihalyi and Nylan 2003 have shown.

This was the term that Sima Tan chose to use in some cases, in his idiosyncratic classification of philosophical tendencies in *Shiji* 130 (cf. Chapter 1, p. 23). Although he did not discuss the transmission of texts, that was often the focus of attention when later writers talked of philosophical groups in terms of *jia*. Certainly admission to such a group generally carried obligations of loyalty, and from the Eastern Han onwards, one of the primary duties was handing on the canonical texts, the *jing*. That did not mean an end to the disagreements that I noted before concerning what the Master stood for. Yet the very term *jia* itself tended to imply a close analogy between the father-son and the master-pupil relationships.

The chief new factor that our Chinese materials introduce into the discussion is the developed examination system that governed entry to and graduation from the Imperial Academy. That had little immediate effect on the ways in which technical knowledge in such fields as medicine and mathematics was handed on, though it certainly channelled the ambitions of those seeking to break into the literate elite. Its impact, in that context, was twofold. On the one hand, as noted, new talent achieved recognition. On the other, the skills by which that talent was judged were closely, if not narrowly, defined in terms of the mastery of the canonical texts. It was only a good deal later, in Tang times, that technical questions in such fields as astronomy and mathematics figured regularly in the speciality examinations that were then set (Elman 2000: 10).

*

If we turn now to our third civilisation, ancient Greece, I have already discussed in Chapter 1 the indefiniteness surrounding three of the more general terms for the learned, namely *sophos*, *sophistês* and *philosophos*. To recapitulate the main points: you could acquire a reputation for being *sophos* (wise, clever) in many different ways, for example by being skilled in an art or craft such as poetry. 'Sophist' is applied especially, though not exclusively, to professional teachers who taught a wide range of subjects for pay, but it is sometimes used to express disapproval whether of the subjects taught or of the motives of the teachers. 'Philosopher', used very generally before Plato, gets to be appropriated by him for the Socratic pursuit of truth as Plato himself construed it. But other views on both the goal and content of 'philosophy' continued to be put forward both from inside and from outside the ranks of the self-styled philosophers themselves.

Meanwhile some of the more specific Greek terms for different learned disciplines have a deceptively familiar ring, and so we must be especially cautious. *Mathêmatikos* is far from confined to those we might consider to be 'mathematicians'. It can be used generally of those who are fond of learning and is often applied to astronomers and astrologers. The terms *astronomos* and *astrologos* themselves do not reliably pick out the distinction we draw between astronomy and astrology (even though that distinction is made, in other terms, for example by Ptolemy).[5] Rather, both terms are often used interchangeably for those who studied the heavens.

The first essential point about the situation in Greece is a negative one, the absence of considerable numbers of official posts to which members of the literate elite might aspire. We cannot, for Greece, give long lists of such positions, as we can for both Mesopotamia and China: we cannot even do so for Rome, even though it did eventually develop something of a bureaucracy. Moreover, as I made clear, scholars did not normally think of the Roman civil service as their natural career.

There are, to be sure, some exceptions. The institutions that the Ptolemies founded in Alexandria, the Museum and the Library, offered some stipendiary positions, not least that of Librarian itself, and other Hellenistic states copied the Ptolemies in this as in other respects. Under the Roman Empire there were eventually endowed Chairs for the main philosophical schools at Athens and other official teaching posts elsewhere. But by the comparative standards we have chosen – those of our other two ancient civilisations – the openings were meagre.

Thus aspiring astronomers and mathematicians generally had to go it alone. Meton, Euctemon and Callippus did not do their work on the calendar as paid civil servants of the city-state of Athens. Indeed their results were often ignored or implemented only after some delay. There were, to be sure, some paid public physicians in the classical period, but appointments were temporary, not permanent. In the famous case of Democedes, recorded by Herodotus (III 129-31), he held positions at Aegina, Athens and Samos, each for a year, in successive years. Eventually in Hellenistic Egypt there were tax immunities for doctors on the so-called *numerus* (quota) and they were subject to evaluation by other doctors, though not by formal written examination (Nutton 1988: chs IV and V). That scrutiny was designed to check their colleagues' respectability as much as their competence. Later still, in the second century CE, moral probity continues to be a factor in Galen's treatise *On the Examination of the Physician*, a work to be used, so he tells his reader, only if a competent doctor cannot be found on the recommendation of trustworthy friends or acquaintances.

The lack of official posts may have had one advantage, namely that the state itself did not oversee new entrants to the discipline. But as the examples I have just cited show, that did not mean there was *no* control, of doctors, at least, even if that was exercised by existing practitioners themselves. Notably the Hippocratic *Oath* lays down how the doctor should behave (again the important issue was morality, not lore), and the *Law* speaks of the importance of not revealing the mysteries of medicine to outsiders. But again those points should not be exaggerated. It is not clear who swore the *Oath*, but it can only have been a sub-set of the literate authors represented in our extant Hippocratic Corpus, since several of them breach the prohibitions that the *Oath* lays down (such as not procuring abortion). While the *Law* thinks of medicine in terms borrowed from religion and as secretive, the author of the treatise *On Ancient Medicine* insists, for his part, that the doctor should make himself intelligible to his patients.

The disagreements among Greek doctors did not relate just to matters of morality or etiquette in medical practice. Disputes over fundamentals, the causes of diseases and methods of treatment, were extremely widespread. They extended even to the issue of whether medicine is indeed a *technê*, an art or rational skill, and if so, what kind – questions that Chinese doctors would never have dreamed of raising. Nor was it just a matter of disagreements between literate doctors and other more marginal types, the root-cutters, drug-sellers, and the misleadingly named midwives (female healers), but also within the literate elite represented in our sources. Following an oblique remark in Galen, modern scholars used to generalise about 'Coan' and 'Cnidian' 'schools of medicine'. Yet the evidence in the history of medicine in Anonymus Londinensis shows that different doctors associated with Cos took very different stands, on pathology, therapeutics and even epistemology, and the same may be said of those who came from Cnidos. There is no way to reconstruct 'Coan' medicine, or 'Cnidian', for there was no such thing.

These disputes had important repercussions on medical training. In the *Protagoras*, 311b ff., Plato implies that someone wanting to study medicine would go, for instance, to Hippocrates to be taught. But though he clearly had a reputation already in his own day, there were plenty of others of whom the same could be said, Euryphon, Philistion, Polybus, Petron of Aegina, even Philolaus, and others named in Anonymus Londinensis. That meant that a student was faced with considerable choice. Although any given teacher would expect loyalty from his pupils, they, for their part, could and some-times did vote with their feet and transfer their allegiances from one physician to another. In the Hellenistic period especially, the three main groups identified by Celsus and Galen, that is the so-called Dogmatists,[6] the Empiricists and the Methodists, were locked in more or less constant dispute with one another on as wide a range of issues as I identified for the Hippocratics. Indeed it was wider, in that it extended also to questions such as the validity of dissection and vivi-section, their usefulness for medical practice and – where human subjects were concerned – their morality.[7] Defection from one leader or group to another was common. To cite just a single example, the founder of the Empiricist sect was Philinus, and he had started out as a follower of Herophilus (rated a 'Dogmatist' by Celsus and Galen).

2. Learned Elites: their Training, Openness and Control

Doctors never needed public appointment in order to practise, since they could make a living from the fees they charged their patients. But mathematicians and astronomers could hardly do the same – not at least until astrology, the casting of horoscopes, became all the rage in the Hellenistic period (Barton 1994). That certainly helped to keep both astronomy and mathematics going in ancient Greece. Many may have been well enough off to avoid having to earn a living. This was a slave-based society, and the arguments of Finley and others, that that was a crucial factor in securing the leisure for even citizens of modest means to engage in otherwise unproductive political and intellectual pursuits, still stand. But for those who did need to make money, teaching was important. So it was too, of course, in Mesopotamia and China, but comparatively speaking its significance was greater in Greece, given the lack of official positions that we have noticed, and given the further fact that patronage was not a well-developed institution in classical Greece either (cf. Lloyd and Sivin 2002: ch. 3).

Our admittedly limited evidence for mathematicians and astronomers in the classical period suggests a varied pattern, with a number combining their interests in those fields with others, for example in philosophy. Hippocrates of Chios may have been an exception. He is said to have been responsible for the first systematisation of mathematical knowledge in a book (now no longer extant) that later sources saw as the forerunner of Euclid's *Elements*. But all we hear about him, other than his achievements in mathematics, was that he was naïve in practical matters.[8] He may have been wealthy to begin with, but he appears to have lost most of his fortune from his foolishness.

Several other prominent early mathematicians, including Philolaus and Archytas, are said to have been Pythagoreans, and here too we have problems with our sources, which tend to exaggerate both the extent and the secretiveness of that group. Late neo-Pythagorean writers make much of the latter characteristic, for obvious reasons. It helped them to ascribe the positions they themselves maintained to Pythagoras himself, despite the lack of direct evidence, for that lack could be put down to the alleged secretiveness.

51

It is clear too from what we know about Empedocles that it was possible to agree with Pythagoras on some issues (such as the transmigration of souls) but to present original ideas in such areas as cosmology. The famous doctrine that 'all things are numbers' is best interpreted, in my opinion, as the view that the explanations of the phenomena are to be found in the quantitative relations that they manifest, as in the case of the principal musical harmonies.

Both Philolaus and Archytas show a particular interest in music theory, though also in many other fields of study. It is striking that they appear to have disagreed on the issue of the hierarchy of the mathematical disciplines. Philolaus is said to have claimed that geometry is the source and metropolis ('mother-city') of mathematics, while Archytas privileged arithmetic. Some of our sources offer a tantalising glimpse of an educational programme that Archytas may have proposed, linking arithmetic, geometry, harmonics and astronomy, in what seems like an anticipation of Plato's propaedeutic studies in the *Republic* – unless, that is, those sources have simply read back Plato's ideas into Archytas. Yet there is this difference, in any event, between Plato and what is ascribed to Archytas, namely that in the latter those mathematical disciplines are undertaken for their own sakes, not just as a preliminary to the study of dialectic, the investigation of the Forms, essential, in Plato's view, for the philosopher-kings.

If the Pythagoreans are an exceptional group, the experience of the most famous early fourth-century mathematician and astronomer may have been closer to a more normal pattern (though it is difficult to talk of such when we are dealing with only a few individuals in any case). This was Eudoxus, renowned both for the mathematical method of exhaustion and for the geometrical model of planetary motion based on concentric spheres. He too, like Philolaus and Archytas, was – as we learn from Diogenes Laertius (VIII 86ff.) – something of a polymath, a physician and law-giver as well as astronomer and geometer. He apparently did have to earn a living and the way he did so is revealing. He went the rounds of several city-states – and even to the court of Mausolus in Caria – picking up pupils. By the time he settled in Athens – joining Plato's Academy indeed – he had a large following. We can only guess what they found attractive in his lectures. It may be that his success owed more to his moral philosophy (where he identified the good with the pleasant)[9] than to his advanced mathematics. But it was clearly as a teacher that he made his reputation in the first place. On the one hand, Greek intellectuals of all types did not generally have to please Emperors or kings. On the other, they did have to attract and hold an audience, and that, one might think, was sometimes just as difficult, even though the skills that demanded were in certain respects rather different. I shall be returning to this issue in my next chapter.

*

My survey has inevitably been highly selective, but it already suggests the complexities of the problems. We have noticed the major differences in the situations that intellectuals of different types faced in different fields and at different periods. One might perhaps have expected that those differences would correlate *either* with features of the civilisation concerned, *or* with the field, as between mathematics, say, or astronomy, or medicine. But what we have found does not support any such correlation unequivocally.

We cannot generalise about Mesopotamian learned elites as a whole, or Chinese ones, or Greek, since the evidence suggests considerable variety within each of those cultures. In all three cases there are differences between those with some claim to be generally learned and those with some technical expertise, and again further differences between those with different such expertises, as specialists in the heavens, or as healers.

Nor if we take the study of the heavens (for instance) can we say that the skills needed to enter the elite circles in question were uniform across these three ancient societies. To start with, the nature of the studies undertaken differed, as too did the relationship between observational and theoretical work, the kinds of theories cultivated, the relationship between what we would call astronomy, and astrology, and above all the roles of the state authorities, in the extent, for example, to which they set the agenda and used the results. Doctors were, no doubt, everywhere faced with broadly similar problems in coping with their patients in antiquity as later. But the training and scrutiny that some doctors underwent varied, as did the public image of confidence they showed about what they were able to achieve.

Seven main factors can be distinguished that are important for access to these elites, namely birth, moral probity, apprenticeship, initiation, mastery of texts, examination, and success in practice. In addition wealth always carried an advantage. Patronage too enabled individuals to cultivate their own interests – provided they met with their patron's approval.

Let me summarise some findings under these seven heads.

(1) Birth is certainly an important factor in all three civilisations, in that many offices and skills were handed down from father to son. Exceptions can, of course, be found, more in China perhaps than in Mesopotamia. In Greece, while birth counted for something among doctors, that is less true of sophists or philosophers or mathematicians.

(2) Being thought to be morally respectable made a difference again in all three civilisations, though how you persuaded people of that varied. In Greece the point applies, again, more to doctors than to mathematicians. Greek philosophers and sophists often claimed moral virtue, in the face of some scepticism in some cases. In China advice on conduct, ranging from personal behaviour to state policies, was a regular part of the counsel offered by philosophers and persuaders of different types, and the acceptability of the advice often depended to some extent on the perceived moral integrity of the adviser.

(3) Some form of apprenticeship is widespread, though naturally that varied with the skills in question. What it meant to learn from a practitioner in medicine would be rather different from being taught divination or astronomy. One may distinguish also between learning some substantive subject, and learning how to become a teacher oneself – as was the case with many Greek philosophers.

(4) In several instances we have evidence of specific rites of initiation, including, for example, the swearing of an oath, before being accepted for training. We found that in some Chinese and Greek medical texts and in Mesopotamian divination. Clearly some special-

ists were keen to claim that their knowledge was special by describing it as secret or exclusive.

(5) The mastery of canonical texts is essential throughout Mesopotamian literate elites and in the Chinese text-based lineages. No such command of canons was a prerequisite in *classical* Greece (there were no such canons), but in Hellenistic times and later the study of the writings of the great names of the past was certainly expected of those who styled themselves their followers, as Platonists, for example, or Hippocrateans, while for mathematicians Euclid's *Elements* provided an essential basic reference text. In late antiquity the writings of Galen came to dominate education in medicine, as did those of Ptolemy in the study of the heavens.

The degree of authoritativeness accorded to the canons varied as between civilisations, periods and fields. The more difficult and esoteric the text, the more its study would need to be supplemented by oral instruction from an existing expert. We know of competing interpretations of Chinese canons (cf. Chapter 1, p. 159n.5): what is exceptional in Greece is the extent to which pupils could pick and choose by whom they wished to be taught.

(6) Formal written examinations on such canonical literature were unique to China from the Han: the scrutiny that doctors entering the *numerus* in Hellenistic Egypt underwent was no test of their mastery of the medical treatises.

(7) The question of perceived success in practice is particularly problematic. When, as in Greece, there were fewer official posts, it was easier for an outsider to break in, if they had the ambition and talent to succeed, but that included the rhetorical talent to persuade others of that. What counted as successful medical practice was often very much in the eyes of the beholder, encouraged, of course, by what the doctor told him or her to behold. In astronomy, getting an eclipse prediction right was eminently verifiable: but if you got it wrong, there was no shortage of excuses to account for that. In mathematics, cracking problems that had defeated everyone else was also objective enough. Yet even in mathematics presentational skills still counted for something. Euclid's *Elements* overwhelmed the reader with the evident incontrovertibility of the results. Demonstration in the

axiomatic-deductive mode was just the most effective tactic of persuasion of all. Of course there was more to the development of that style of reasoning in Greece than just presentation. Yet we should acknowledge that it was one factor in play. In other fields, too, the Greek preoccupation with second-order questions, with epistemology, with methodology, with foundations, can also be related to a certain need not just to get the answer right, but to be seen incontestably to have got it right. The fact that in other ancient civilisations those preoccupations were far less prominent (and the ambition to produce axiomatic-deductive demonstration non-existent) reflects, paradoxically it may be, the greater self-confidence or security of the learned elites in those civilisations.

This takes me to my final point before I turn to the modern world. Learned elites often respond to the needs of the state, but they can and do emerge independently of those needs. The very fact that the members of the groups in question see themselves or are seen by others as distinctive marks them out, but the barriers to entry varied greatly both in type and in scale. The Greek 'sophists' are exceptional in that just about anyone could, in principle, set themselves up as one. They may be exceptionally controversial, in that the label could be used pejoratively (but so too could the Chinese term *ru*) and those so labelled attracted severe criticism, at least in some certain quarters.

That might suggest that the easier the access to the elite group, the more difficult it was for its members to achieve uniform respectability. The more official the functions of the posts assumed, the more immune to some types of external criticism their incumbents could be. No one could deny that someone held the position of 'chief scribe' or *taishi ling*, though whether they deserved to do so was another matter. Yet that did not stop individual members of many groups from criticising their own colleagues, as Babylonian scribes criticise other scribes, or Chinese *ru* criticise other *ru*. The analysis of the argumentative schemata employed in such polemics – with the focus sometimes on morality, sometimes on method, sometimes on results – reflects the degree and nature of the vulnerability of individuals within the group as also of its cohesiveness and sense of solidarity.

2. Learned Elites: their Training, Openness and Control

*

Let me now once again stand back and ask some similar questions about our present situation. How far are we able to do any better in our methods of recruitment to, and regulation of, our learned elites? How far do we achieve an optimum balance between the need to ensure professional competence and allowing originality to flourish? The topic is admittedly a vast one, but our survey of ancient civilisations prompts some tentative observations.

Ever since the Middle Ages in Europe entry to the learned professions – initially there were just the three, law, medicine and theology – has been jealously guarded. Universities were generally for the well-to-do or for those fortunate enough to find a patron. Students had to be competent in Latin and (like their counterparts in the much earlier Chinese Imperial Academy) to be of good character. A relic of that is to be found in the formula still used by Cambridge Colleges when presenting their students for degrees, when they are vouched for as to their behaviour (*mores*) as well as for having passed their examinations (*doctrina*): '*quos scio tam moribus quam doctrina esse idoneos ad gradum assequendum*'. These are ceremonial occasions and Latin is still considered appropriate.

During the twentieth century dramatic changes took place in opening up the universities and the professions to which they led. It may have taken several hundred years for the older British universities to admit women, and even then at first they were not permitted to take degrees, but eventually it did happen. With the Butler Act of 1945 those who won a place at university were assured of a grant and the proportion of those from state schools increased. Yet if these were changes for the better, there is still a long way to go. The under-representation of women in the professions and in the universities themselves is still a scandal. Entry to university is still not perceived to be *solely* on merit, for the older ones are still thought of as largely for the privileged. The recent reversal of the policies that animated the Butler Act – principally that of free university education – has meant that once again the less well-to-do are deterred.

In other ways, too, the universities have proved to be, in general, highly conservative institutions. Curriculum change, painfully slow during the eighteenth and nineteenth centuries, is still laborious. The point can be illustrated for medicine, even, in that it was only well into the nineteenth century that the ancient Greek medical authors, 'Hippocrates' and Galen, ceased to be a compulsory part of the course at Oxford. A study of the examination papers set for the BA degree in Cambridge shows how slow they are to change: the same or very similar questions figure year after year, not only in a subject such as philosophy, but even in physiology.

University professors still have a tendency to teach their subjects in very much the same way as they were taught them. They appreciate, in their students, precisely those qualities that gave them their own success. Lip-service is certainly given to the value of originality. But that is a dangerous talent to display too soon in one's career, since it may well mean failing to gain the top qualifications needed to pass on to the next stage of study. Spotting true originality in undergraduates is admittedly difficult: the argument that they must first show that they have mastered the state of the field as it currently exists has some validity. But it is regrettably the case that much innovative work done by undergraduates and in graduate dissertations encounters resistance among examiners.

But is it not the case that, once a student has passed through all the hoops and is launched on a career, there is every chance that talent will be duly rewarded? One strength of the current situation is that in most subjects there are plenty of different outlets for publication – journals and publishing houses – to which papers or manuscripts can be submitted.[10] There is usually a recognised pecking order among these, so that papers in the top journals will count for more on a person's CV than those in lesser publications. But at least the boards of referees will not be identical for all, and what is turned down by one may be accepted by another.

Yet major scientific breakthroughs, when they come, still meet resistance. The reception of the new ideas associated with plate tectonics and with the discovery of the structure of DNA illustrates this vividly. In Cambridge, in both cases, the principal proponents were, to start with, treated with suspicion, even hostility, and their

58

scientific credentials were called into question. There has, to be sure, been a good deal of retrospective rewriting of the history of both revolutions – including by the proponents themselves. But it is agreed on all sides that the existing scientific establishment initially not only did not welcome Crick and Watson, but were at points obstructive.

Pluralism – the possibility of different approaches – has clearly been a major factor in achieving progress in many subjects. I celebrated philosophical pluralism in Chapter 1. The existence of different scientific groups pursuing their own programmes, developing new lines of inquiry into existing fields and branching out into new ones, is no doubt crucial to scientific exploration and advance. The experience of ancient Greece already shows how fruitful in stimulating new ideas a pluralist, competitive environment can be, even though many of the ideas in question, such as heliocentricity, were stillborn there, and even though the institutional support – even for the proposals the Greeks themselves thought most worthwhile – was minimal. In many ways and in many areas the situation in China was the converse, strong state support for the favoured programme, but often insufficient discussion of alternatives. It is only in the modern world, since the nineteenth century, that the perceived importance of science has ensured a massive devotion of resources to its development, allowing pluralism unprecedented scope.

Yet the motives that underpin that massive investment in science are not just those of the disinterested pursuit of the truth, to be sure. Commercial, as well as military, goals are increasingly important factors in determining what research gets done – in the universities themselves, let alone in laboratories dedicated to those ends. In one respect we there need more openness, especially when some product or technique that could benefit humankind in general is exploited almost exclusively for the profit of the company that won the race to patent it first.

On the other hand, when pluralism is a slogan invoked to support a policy of no interference, there are obvious dangers. Of course the idea of any kind of control over scientific programmes is anathema to many. But such an attitude now seems hopelessly idealistic, as more and more scientific work poses deep moral and ethical problems.

59

Those relate not just to the question of the use of animal, and indeed human, subjects for research, but to the unproven risks of genetic engineering in general and to the moral issues raised by human genetic manipulation in particular. There one repeatedly hears the argument that if one laboratory does not do the work, another will, precisely because of the competitive, pluralist environment within which they all work. If there is an embargo on the research in one country, others may well permit it: so why should any country seek to restrict it?

The moral issues that have to be faced do not necessarily lead to the conclusion that there should be a single international body set up to monitor and control scientific research world-wide. Yet there is an urgent need for more international discussion – and not just among the scientific community itself – as to the guidelines that should apply. Then when rules can be agreed, it will take, as it already does take, great determination to implement them, in the face of the pressures of those intent on commercial exploitation. The problem in the modern situation does not lie with pluralism or openness or competitiveness as such, but rather with the values that have driven and will continue to drive research, where the pure pursuit of knowledge sits uneasily with ruthless materialism.

The problems we face are not just modern ones. Aggressive materialism existed in all three ancient civilisations we considered. The issue of the morality of research surfaced in a dramatic way in relation to human vivisection in Hellenistic Alexandria. There was an uneasy tension, in all three civilisations, between secretiveness and transparency, between exclusiveness and openness to new ideas, between the defensiveness of the existing cadres and the ambitions of those who sought to break into them, between government indifference and government control. But if none of the problems is new, their scale today certainly is. In particular, the possibilities for exploiting research, for intervening on, controlling and indeed destroying, the environment, that exist nowadays, are altogether beyond ancient imagining. But if there are no easy solutions, and certainly antiquity cannot provide any, reflection on the ancient world may, nevertheless, serve to highlight the dangers that we face.

2. Learned Elites: their Training, Openness and Control

A historical perspective certainly underlines the need for an awareness of those risks, and for a greater sense of collective responsibility in meeting the challenge they present.

3

Audiences and Assemblies

'*ô andres athênaioi*', 'O Athenian men', is how many classical Athenian political and forensic speeches begin, or when before one of the many jury-courts, '*ô andres dikastai*', where 'gentlemen of the jury' does not quite hit the right note, though for sure the jurors/judges were men. 'Your servant has heard', 'your servant, risking death, wishes to suggest', are common forms of address for Chinese memorials submitted to the Emperor. 'Friends, Romans, Countrymen', Shakespeare's Mark Antony begins, in the task of swaying the mob at Caesar's funeral. 'Mr' or 'Madam' 'Speaker', says the British Prime Minister, and this is how the American President is introduced when he makes his State of the Union speech. We are all aware that conventions of address differ. Automatically we adjust to what we know or think to be appropriate, and on travels, and even sometimes at home, it is wise, in unfamiliar situations, to check what the correct form of address is.

But address is just one feature of decorum in speech. Winning audiences round is a matter of adjusting the persona of yourself that you wish to present, as well as one of knowing your audience through and through. Since Perelman and Olbrechts-Tyteca in Europe, and Marshall McLuhan in North America, the rhetoric that was frowned on by high-minded custodians of the public conscience in earlier centuries has made a come-back.[1] Well beyond classes in communication studies, beyond those in literature indeed, we are taught that the manner of communication influences the content of what is communicated. Or as the slogan has it: the medium is the message.

The two-fold task that this study sets itself follows the pattern of my other investigations. The first task is historical, to undertake a comparative analysis of the primary contexts of the presentation and dissemination of ideas, political, philosophical, scientific, literary, in ancient Greece and China. Who were the audiences that the authors had in mind, in their imagination and in real life? What difference did a difference in audience make to what could be presented and to how to present it? Whom did the authors need to persuade and did they adopt specific tactics in specific contexts to do so? For both classical and Hellenistic Greece, and Warring States and Imperial China, the evidence, though lacunose and skewed by certain biases, is very rich. What light can we throw on the political experience and intellectual products of those civilisations and periods by examining the specificities of the contexts of the production and dissemination of ideas?

The second complementary task is to reflect critically on current practices – in a modern world where the balance between the written and the spoken word has swung back towards the spoken, and where more fundamentally the balance between word and image has moved very much in favour of the latter. Yet the conventions of speeches to different groups still matter, though what is said at a Party meeting (for example) will also address the wider audience to whom the proceedings are reported, even if in sound-bite form, on the TV news programmes or in the papers. In a power-point presentation the main work may be done by the graphics, but certain heads of argument may also be flashed up in a frame – for the audience to read. Indeed the presenter may read them out, to give the audience time to do so, when the texts acquire a double authority: they are spoken, but they are also seen. They remain as markers: but it is the visual images used, with all their immediacy, that do most of the work of persuasion – in a very different way from the way in which words by themselves used to have to perform that function in an old fashioned purely verbal disquisition. It is far easier, after all, to pick out a word or phrase and challenge it than it is to challenge the validity of a picture or the reasons for its selection among many hundreds of others.

*

From the start of Greek literature, the primary function of most work was to entertain. There is some debate over the original contexts of performance of epic poetry, but that the *Iliad* and the *Odyssey* and the other no longer extant works of the Epic Cycle were performed is clear. By the time we get to the classical period, we have a fair bit of evidence relating to the rhapsodes whose job it was to perform epic poetry on formal occasions – for example at the Olympic Games – and at informal ones.

Of course entertainment was not incompatible with other functions. They might include memorialisation – keeping alive ideas about the past, including myths about heroic times when things were very different – and celebrations also of the present – praise of present members of glorious families or just those who sponsored the poem or the poet. Those functions might also and especially include instruction, a feature often of both epic and lyric as well as of the genre we name as specifically didactic, represented pre-eminently by Hesiod's *Theogony* and his *Works and Days*. There the poet tells you what to do and what not to do, on each day of the month, as well as advising about such matters as the best wood for the different parts of a plough (*Works and Days* 427ff.). The instruction spills over into admonition and moralising, as Hesiod warns his brother Perses of the dire consequences (as he claims) of incorrect or unjust behaviour.

The tensions between the different functions that poetry can serve, and between the poet himself and the patrons who sponsored him, emerge more strongly in lyric. The Epinician Ode is a victory celebration for winning in the Olympic or other games, composed for performance either just after the event or, more often, when the winner returned to his home city. But it often seems that the athlete, even the athlete's celebrated family, provide not so much the central subject, as a pretext, for poetic explorations. They receive obligatory honourable mention, but mythical themes may be developed far beyond any conceivable direct relevance to the victory. The patrons get value for money, in those circumstances, not from hearing their praises sung directly, but by being associated, as patron indeed, with a poet recognised for skills that far transcended a gift for flattery.

The existence of a potential audience for instruction opened up the possibility for other genres, including, eventually, those that did not exploit the attractions, and easy memorability, of poetry, but employed prose, relying primarily on the interest and importance of the contents to hold an audience. As I noted before, some early Presocratic philosophers continued to use poetry (Xenophanes, Parmenides, Empedocles), but others provide some of our earliest examples of prose works, even though their style or rather terminology was thought by some later Greek critics to be rather poetic in character (Simplicius on Anaximander). Heraclitus' tactic, to gain and hold attention, was to exploit paradox in terse, apophthegmatic dicta. By the late fifth century a number of prose styles had been developed, some specialised and even esoteric ones conveying technical information to particular groups (as in the case of some of the medical treatises in the Hippocratic Corpus). Again Herodotus' remarkable 'histories', intended certainly for a general audience, set themselves a task – of memorialising – that has obvious affinities with the memorialising ambitions stated at the start of the *Iliad* and the *Odyssey* – though to represent Herodotus as prose epic would be to overdo it.

This takes us to the next important development, beyond literature as entertainment and even literature as instruction. This relates to literature as descriptive record. The speeches and exchanges in Herodotus are no doubt very largely his fabrications. In some cases he invents an encounter that could, for chronological reasons, never have taken place. Yet he evidently wanted to stay close to what it was plausible for Themistocles, or Xerxes, or even Darius, to have said on the specific occasions he described. What was said to persuade the Greeks to fight at Salamis, and what weighed with the Persians in deciding to attack, is presented as description, even though it represents more or less conscientiously researched interpretation.

Thucydides, for his part, explicitly tells us (I 22) that the speeches he puts into the mouths of the principal actors in his history correspond to what it was appropriate for them to have said in the circumstances in question, rather than being a verbatim account of what they actually said. Yet Thucydides, writing about events he lived through himself, was obviously in a far better position than Herodotus had been to report what was said, as he or others remembered it, even though there was no transcript for him to consult. In his account of the Mytilenean debate (III 36ff.) for instance,

Thucydides selects just two spokesmen, one for each of the opposing points of view. Cleon advocates punitive measures against the entire population of the now defeated rebel city of Mytilene, and Diodotus urges leniency, on the grounds that not all were equally guilty of instigating the revolt, and on the further argument of the damage it will do to Athens' relations with its other allies if they take the revenge that Cleon suggested, killing all the male adults and selling the women and children into slavery. Thucydides gives us his version of what happened at the two Assemblies that discussed what to do, on successive days, and he makes the most of the drama of the situation, where first Cleon's side, then Diodotus', wins the day.

There is no way in which we can now recover 'what actually happened' at either of those Assemblies, and in any case there can never be a 'full' account of what happened, even when transcripts are available, since the words themselves do not convey everything that is communicated. Thucydides has been drastically selective and used his best judgement in interpreting the dynamics of the debate. Yet assuming (as I would) that he did not totally invent those debates, and that they did indeed occur, then we can at least say one thing for sure, namely that the Athenians who attended them had to exercise *their* judgement about what was said, about what to say themselves in some cases, and then about how to vote. They had to weigh up the rights and wrongs, and the expediency, of the opposing points of view. Different individuals would, no doubt, pay more or less attention to different considerations, their own reputations, their sense of the motivations that weighed with those who took one or other line, their assessments of the repercussions of speaking and voting in one sense or the other on their own and other political alliances, friendships and vendettas, within the citizen body.[2]

With the extant forensic and political oratory of the fifth and fourth centuries we can get a step closer to, though we still fall short of, actual reportage. The speeches that have come down to us comprise different types of materials. Some, such as the *Tetralogies* of Antiphon, are model speeches providing instruction in the kinds of argument that might be used by prosecution or defence in various types of case. Others invent concrete, but fictional, settings as a framework for political commentary. Thus the *Against Alcibiades*, ascribed to Andocides, purports to represent a speech in favour of ostracising Alcibiades, but it could not have been delivered in the form in which we have it. The speeches of Isocrates provide other examples where the situation is real enough, even though Isocrates himself never delivered them. These aim at a multi-layered readership, in the first instance his own contemporaries (who may, however, have read them or had them read out loud), but beyond them doubtless also prospective future readerships interested in the affairs of state Isocrates discusses, down to ourselves.

Yet a further category represents actual speeches that were given in the circumstances described, to the Assembly, the Council, the Areopagus or other Courts. The full title of one of Lysias' speeches claims that he gave it in person *Against Eratosthenes*, who had been one of the Thirty Tyrants, and it may well broadly correspond to one delivered in 403 BCE. Some of his other speeches were written for others to deliver and again this may well have happened. Thus the work *On the Murder of Eratosthenes* (not the same Eratosthenes) was written for, and given by, the defendant in that case, a man named Euphiletus. In the case of Aeschines' *Against Ctesiphon* and Demosthenes' *On the Crown* we have two speeches from the same trial, addressing the same court on the same issue, of the legality of Ctesiphon's proposal to award a crown to Demosthenes. The case was heard in 330, and Demosthenes himself undertook to speak on behalf of the defendant Ctesiphon. In those instances, and in the vast majority of others, the speech as it has come down to us has been subject to more or less extensive reworking or 'editing for publication' after the event. Yet they remain close to what was said, closer than the *Apologies* for Socrates, written by Xenophon and by Plato, which allow themselves far greater freedom to invent what Socrates said to suit the later, posthumous, defence of his character that those authors proposed.

I shall have more to say about levels of audience and the interactions between actual and imagined ones, in due course, but I must first mention three other Greek genres where there is a more or less close link between literary genre and social institution or practice.

These are symposia, literary or philosophical dialogues, and *epideixeis* or exhibition lectures.

I shall be brief about symposia. They were an aristocratic or at least an oligarchic institution, that from time to time played a significant political role. They did so in connection, for example, with the organisation of *hetaireiai*, political pressure groups active in Athens and other cities. But symposia were the occasion for poetic performance as well as political hobnobbing and homosexual bonding. Various types of lyric poetry were composed for actual or imagined symposia: we have one example in Xenophanes. Then from Plato onwards the symposium came to provide the frame for certain prose works, in which more or less serious topics were discussed in the setting of a symposium. Authors could thus exploit the actual conventions of symposia for their own literary purposes, aware that their own audiences or readership would recognise the social and political undertones of the literary frame.

The link between dialogue as literary form and ordinary conversation is looser, but there are still important factors in the choice of the former as a vehicle for the presentation of ideas that depend upon the conventions of the latter. Plato, of course, is a master of the genre. Socrates, we know from our other evidence too, was notorious for buttonholing anyone he encountered and engaging them in conversation about their personal or political or even unrecognised metaphysical beliefs. The upshot of those conversations, as Plato represents them, is that Socrates' unfortunate interlocutors are shown to be confused and ignorant on subjects they initially pronounced on with the greatest confidence. Not just their words, but also their behaviour, as described in the dialogue, reveal their discomfiture: they sometimes lose their temper or show their petulance by refusing to carry on the conversation.

All of this is very 'true to life', as we may say, but the rules of the game, as Plato sets them up, introduce an asymmetry in what we are told about the interlocutors' views and what we gather about Socrates' own. The interlocutors are generally led into self-contradiction and confess themselves baffled. Socrates, who in any case repeatedly professes his own ignorance, is not usually himself on the receiving end of an equivalent cross-examination. Of course we all recognise, in our own conversational exchanges with others, that they often end in a situation where we are in some doubt about what precisely our friends or acquaintances are committed to. But the systematic indeterminacy of Socrates' own position is a device that Plato uses to engage the reader in far more work in interpretation than would be the case had Socrates (or Plato) presented his ideas in the form of a treatise or even as a single sustained systematic argument.

The reader is taken through the weaknesses of Socrates' interlocutors' opinions, but has to engage in his or her own right in the exploration of Socrates' – or Plato's – own. The art, thereby, of the dialogue form was to mirror, so it seems, actual conversations, but also to propel the reader into further, unscripted, dialogue with Plato himself. What precisely should we take Plato to be committed to? Socrates is always in conversation with this or that individual, with their own presuppositions. But what were Plato's own beliefs on important topics as he would have stated them when *not* representing Socrates cross-examining others? It is not as if interpreters of Plato have finished the task. And it should also be said that no one, after him, made such potent use of the apparently innocent dialogue form, though many tried.

The third genre I mentioned is that of the *epideixis* or exhibition lecture. As with forensic oratory, we have a range of types, and some independent information on the occasions on which such lectures were actually delivered. We can identify some four different, but overlapping, types. When Aristotle classifies the different kinds of rhetoric at *Rhetoric* 1358b6ff., he associates epideictic especially with the oratory of praise and blame. We have one example in Gorgias' *Encomium of Helen*, but that certainly combines a second function with the overt primary one of praising Helen. Both the *Helen* and the *Defence of Palamedes* are tours de force, in which Gorgias takes seemingly hopeless causes – that Helen was not responsible for her actions, and the innocence of the traitor Palamedes – and with a series of brilliant, if at points captious, arguments shows that the common view is wrong and his own, counter-intuitive, thesis correct.

The second function an *epideixis* may serve is, then, as a display of brilliance in speaking, but that in turn may overlap with a further quite specific aim, namely to attract pupils. Many of those whom Plato labels 'sophists' gave lectures, which themselves might or might not be free, where part of the aim was to get some of those in the audience to attend more elaborate courses for which there would indeed be a charge. We hear that Prodicus had both a one-drachma and a fifty-drachma *epideixis* on the correctness of names (*Cratylus* 384bc) and Aristotle, *Rhetoric* 1415b15ff., says that he occasionally spiced the cheaper version with excerpts from the more expensive, if he thought his audience's attention was wandering.

Prodicus' lectures would be of general interest, as indeed would most *epideixeis*. But we should not underestimate the technical detail that was sometimes included – so this is the fourth possible function for the genre. We can see this especially in the medical treatises that refer to, and themselves sometimes exemplify, the epideictic genre. *On the Art* – itself quite likely to be an *epideixis* – talks of those who make a living out of vilifying the arts, including medicine. We can imagine set pieces arguing for this paradoxical conclusion much in the way that Gorgias' *Helen* and *Palamedes* argue for theirs. *On the Nature of Man* speaks of those who discussed such questions as the constituent elements of the human body, apparently in front of a lay audience who adjudicated who had won the debate. Here too there is an interesting relationship between the lectures this treatise criticises and the treatise itself. While the author disagrees with the monistic position of the various groups of theorists – not all doctors – who broached the subjects he mentions, his own exposition of his pluralist element theory has many of the marks of an *epideixis* (cf. Lloyd 1979: 92-4). Thus the contents of what was offered as an *epideixis* could vary from a display of argumentative virtuosity for its own sake, to quite detailed expositions of technical materials.

So too the occasions on which *epideixeis* were given vary. We hear from Plato that Hippias and Gorgias gave *epideixeis* at the Olympic and Pythian games, and indeed that they followed up their speeches with question and answer sessions, in which they were prepared to tackle any subject that anyone cared to propose. Isocrates, too, in his letter to Dionysius I, says that the festivals are suitable occasions for those seeking to make a display (in an *epideixis*) 'for there in the presence of great numbers of people they may spread the fame of their talents abroad'. But while the Games provided grand occasions for *epideixeis*, the sophists and others sometimes operated in less formal contexts. Plato's *Protagoras* (314e ff.) describes a meeting in Callias' house, where a great crowd had gathered, Athenians and others, to hear three of the most notable sophists, Protagoras, Hippias and Prodicus. That account is no doubt fictitious: but it represents the less formal end of the spectrum of possible contexts in which display speeches were given.

There are many other genres of literature that we might consider, but it is time now to return to the issue of levels of audience. In classical Greece we can distinguish at least three primary audiences: first, those who were present in the Assemblies, Councils, or law-courts when important matters were discussed; second, the contemporary audience of those who described such meetings; and third, the further, future, audience those authors had in mind in the works they composed.

The overlap and interaction between these levels, the first two especially, are considerable. It is well known that fifth-century BCE Greece was still a culture in which most exchanges were in the oral mode, and literature when it was read, was still often read out.[3] But more than that: a good deal of the extant literature from that period is *about* oral communication. Most Greeks would have had plenty of experience of both roles in the communicative process, as senders and persuaders, on the one side, as receivers and the objects of persuasion, on the other. Again, the very same citizens who evaluated the arguments and took the decisions in the Assemblies and law-courts were also the contemporary audience for those who wrote up those occasions, whether as historians or as the authors of our extant political and forensic oratory.

In the Assembly of a democratic city such as Athens the crucial principles were that anyone had the right to speak, *isêgoria*, and when it came to taking a decision, everyone's vote counted as equal. The audience on those occasions was not there as literary critics, judging the finer points of style. They had to decide what was for the good of the city – their city – just as it was their votes in the law-courts that found defendants guilty or not guilty and maybe sentenced the former to death. Those duties concentrated the mind, even if many (elite) critics of the democracy said that it behaved with consistent irresponsibility. Listening to the speeches that were made gave them, as I said, a fair amount of experience, in judging the honesty and motivations of the speakers, and in evaluating the arguments and evidence they adduced. After all, members of that primary audience, in their other role as speakers themselves, were well used to thinking about how to make the best of the cases they needed to present.

But then at the second level, some of these same citizens were the contemporary audience for the works that circulated after the event, both the more imaginative reconstructions of Thucydides' speeches and Plato's and Xenophon's version of Socrates' Defence, and what purport to be the actual speeches of some of the orators themselves. Aeschines in *Against Ctesiphon* and Demosthenes *On the Crown* thus each had, in a way, a second chance to persuade people of the validity of their point of view, and this time those readers could judge what they had said undistracted by the actual complex emotions of the live debate. The people who constituted that second audience not only may have belonged also to the first, but may still have been active, many of them, in the political scene. Aeschines, having lost the vote on the crown, retired from Athens: yet he still produced the text of his speech for the record.

For us, the third audience of today, this is all, as we say, past history. Yet history is never fully past, not at least when we use it to learn about the present, in two ways especially. First we may continue to reflect on the rights and wrongs, the successes and failures, of particular policies, on the reasons they were adopted, and on why they succeeded or failed. Secondly, at a different level, we may attempt, as I am doing, to explore the implications of different types of communicative exchange, and the effect of different kinds of audience/speaker interaction, on the nature of what was communicated.

Detienne and his collaborators (2003) have investigated the institution of the Assembly cross-culturally, and analysed how they have worked in different cultures in different periods. They have produced some interesting present-day examples and demonstrated both the frequency and heterogeneity of Assemblies. Some have elaborate formal rules and conventions, others make do with a minimum of such. Some exhibit prominent hierarchical features, others are strongly egalitarian, and this may be so even in societies in which power and authority are otherwise unevenly distributed. Again there are important differences in the scope of what the Assembly can discuss and in the manner in which decisions are made and implemented.

All of this goes to show that the institutions we have been discussing from Greece from the Homeric to the classical period are far from unique. What Detienne's analysis brings to light, by contrast, is, however, first the exceptional intensity of political participation in the classical city-state and secondly the degree to which the models of the political Assembly and law-court were followed or invoked in other domains of intellectual activity as well. I have remarked, in connection with the *epideixis* genre, that lectures were sometimes not solo performances, but belonged to a series of debates, where rival points of view were presented by different speakers. This tended to turn the occasion into a contest, which the audience adjudicated just as it would if trying a court case or voting in the Assembly.

This slippage or interaction between the political and the more purely intellectual spheres is the occasion of comment by the Greeks themselves. Thucydides has Cleon remark, in the Mytilenean debate of 427, that the members of the Assembly were not treating their responsibilities with the seriousness they deserved. Everyone wants to be an orator, he says: everyone wants to be known for the quickness of their wit, praising sharp remarks before they are out of someone's mouth. They behave, as he puts it (III 37ff., 38.7) more like an audience at a performance of sophists, than like people deliberating on affairs of state.

Meanwhile we know that Plato, for his part, condemned politicians and sophists for each, in their own way, playing to their audiences. The goal they set themselves was mere persuasion – while Plato demanded that philosophical inquiry should deliver the truth, indeed demonstrate it. But if this new notion of demonstration, developed

74

first by Plato and then by Aristotle, was to prove extremely influential for subsequent Greek philosophy, mathematics and science, we should not forget what it owed to the *negative* models of persuasion exemplified in the Assemblies, law-courts and sophistic *epideixeis*. The arguments of the statesmen and sophists showed what to avoid – in Plato's view. Persuasion was not enough. It is typical and significant that in the *Gorgias* Socrates is made to insist that he does not have any other audience to convince, only himself. His aim is the truth, and the truth is never refuted (*Gorgias* 473b).

*

How far is it possible to identify the main or prominent contexts of intellectual exchange in ancient China, and do they have a traceable influence on the content of those exchanges and on the modes of intellectual development more generally? The situation of teachers and advisers in China in the Warring States period is, at least in some respects, similar to their Greek counterparts of the classical period. Just as Greek sophists, doctors and others moved from one city-state to another, so many Chinese intellectuals of the Warring States period are reported as active in many other states besides where they happened to be born. The term *youshui* was used of these 'itinerant advisers', and 'itinerant' was, indeed, what most of them were. Confucius, based at times in his home state of Lu, travelled extensively in search of a ruler worthy of his advice, and the same is true of Mozi, Mencius, Gongsun Long, Xunzi and many others. After the unification, to be sure, the opportunity to try your luck with different patrons declined. You had rather to concentrate on the Emperor and his court.

A second feature of similarity with Greece is that each of the most famous of the early Chinese thinkers collected an entourage of pupils. How extensive these were is difficult to judge. *Huainanzi*, written more than three hundred years after Confucius, reports that he had seventy disciples and 3000 followers, while Mozi had 180 (XX 14B). Less plausibly, it credits Gongsun Long with quite a following too (XII 15B). While the actual numbers cannot be confirmed, the general message is clear. Again, in the *Lunyu* ascribed to Confucius but compiled by his followers, he is represented as in dialogue with various of his close associates, Yan Hui, Ran You, Zilu, Zigong, Zixia and the rest. Their roles might, at a pinch, be compared with those of Glaucon and Adeimantus in the *Republic*, or Simmias and Cebes in the *Phaedo*. The *Lunyu* also brings Confucius into confrontation with unsympathetic, if not positively hostile, notables, including members of the influential, but opportunistic Ji family, although he never faces anyone quite like Thrasymachus or Callicles. In the *Zhuangzi* (29), however, we have a delicious satirical representation of Confucius in audience with the famous robber Zhi. On one occasion in the *Lunyu* (2.5ff.) Confucius is asked the same question, about the nature of filial piety, by four different people, Meng Yi Zi, Meng Wu Bo and two of his own disciples, Ziyou and Zixia, and he replies differently to each. We are to understand that the lesson Confucius wishes to convey is tailored to the person to whom he is conveying it.[4]

A third similarity, relating to debate, will take us to a fundamental point of contrast with ancient Greece. We have ample evidence, in the *Zhanguoce*[5] and the *Shiji* especially, for the discussions that were held between rulers and their advisers. We may distinguish, on the one hand, affairs of state, military matters, alliances and the like, and on the other, more general intellectual or cultural issues, to do with cosmology, for instance, or astronomy or the calendar, even though in China those too tended to have political repercussions and significance.

I have underlined before the cardinal importance of the question of good government as the topic on which Chinese philosophers wanted, above all, to advise rulers. Sometimes they did so by soliciting an audi-ence: or, more often it would appear, they submitted a memorial to the throne. When Chief Minister Wang Man, Imperial Secretary Feng Jie and Superintendent of Trials Li Si are consulted on the proper title for the king of Qin after he had successfully completed the unification of China, the *Shiji* (Annals of Qin) records their reply. 'Your servants have carefully discussed this with the scholars of broad learning (*boshi*) and as in antiquity there was the Heavenly August, the Earthly August and the Supreme August, and the Supreme August was the most highly honoured, so your servants, risking death, submit a venerable title and propose that the king should become "the Supreme August" ' (6, 236: 5ff., trans. Dawson 1994: 64). Again when Li Si (by now Chief Minister) submitted his memorial proposing, notoriously, the burning of most privately owned literature, he again uses the conventional formula (6, 255: 2): 'As chief minister, your servant Li Si speaks out at risk of death ....'

On any occasion of any importance the ruler would naturally pay careful attention to the advice he was given and no doubt he would consult all his most trusted ministers on the issues. But the key point is that he alone ultimately decided. The debate was advisory but there was never any question of counting votes at the end of it. The advisers, for their part, knew precisely whom they had to persuade. The situation was evidently very different from that of any classical Greek statesman or sophist who wanted to influence political decisions – although it has, to be sure, close analogies with that of those who set out to influence Roman Emperors. True, at Athens, Pericles was, as I noted before, by far the most important political leader, being re-elected general on many occasions. Yet even Pericles did not always have his own way. Thucydides records (II 65) that in 430 the Athenians were in some despair at the ravages the Spartans were causing in their invasions of Attica, and at the outbreak of plague in the city: they blamed Pericles' policies for their misfortunes – his insistence that they stay within the walls and not take the Spartans on in a pitched battle. To express their disapproval, they deposed and fined him. His position was clearly very different from that of the rulers of any of the Chinese Warring States, let alone from that of Qin Shi Huang Di after the unification. None of them had an Assembly to win round to approve their policies: none of them was subject to re-election.

The second category of debate I distinguished relates not to affairs of state, but to such areas as cosmology or astronomy. We have evidence in the *Hou Hanshu* treatise 2: 3025ff., for instance, of a remarkable sequence of discussions to do with calendrical computation, starting in 68 CE and continuing for more than a hundred years. The two modern specialists in the field who have reviewed this material have chosen, interestingly, each to emphasise a different aspect of it. Cullen 2000 has stressed the importance of the fact that open discussions were held between competing points of view. One such debate, recorded in a memorial of Jia Kui in 92 (*Hou Hanshu* 3027-30), relates to whether the Yellow Road (that is, the ecliptic) or the Red Road (the equator) is the better basis for calculating the movements of the sun and moon. Against the opinions of certain astronomical officials, the view Jia Kui himself favoured, namely that the ecliptic was preferable, prevailed, even though some complained that it was hard to use in practice.

Then in the mid-130s Zhang Heng worked out a method for converting movement along the ecliptic to movement on the equator. Yet his reforms met with greater resistance. Cullen notes that 'the reality of power at court was shown very clearly when in the presence of a group of eunuchs the Emperor asked Zhang Heng who were the most detested persons in the Empire: under their malevolent gaze he found that he dared not speak the truth that was in his mind, and not long afterwards left the capital for a provincial posting' (*Hou Hanshu* 59: 1914).

It is precisely the politics of the infighting at court that the other modern expert in this field has focused on. Sivin (in Lloyd and Sivin 2002: 78) has examined an account of discussions in 175 CE in *Hou Hanshu* 3037-40 that concerned 'a charge by two officials that errors in the current astronomical system were responsible for a rebellion'. An edict ordered high palace officials to meet in the Office of the Minister of Education. The report describes how blocks of officials of varying ranks were drawn up on all four sides of a courtyard with a clerk seated in the middle to read the imperial edict. An eminent Court Gentleman for Consultation (Cai Yong) refuted the complainants' arguments in detail, despite their being comparatively junior. Since their charge cast doubt on the Emperor's mandate (rebellion being a portent of misrule), three high officials indicted them for *lèse-majesté* and recommended that they be punished. However, thanks to a further imperial edict the case was dropped.

Here then, even though the topic of the conference was, at one level, a matter of calendrical administration, and as such a technical issue, that was not all it was. In the Greek instances I discussed there was some slippage between styles of debate, as between those of intellectual exchange and those of the Greek law-courts. But this, Chinese, legal process was held in no Dicastery (where there were large numbers of citizens chosen by lot and acting as both judge and jury). This was a Chinese court, with the full panoply of the imperial administration there to see that the Emperor's wishes – as inter-preted – were carried out. Although technical discussions were held, the final say rested with the Emperor or his officials.

The fact that decisions on most important questions, whether directly political, or intellectual and cultural, were taken centrally gave a very sharp focus to attempts to influence them. There was plenty of opportunity to exercise skills in persuasion. But normally they would be wasted, if not aimed, directly or indirectly, at swaying the views of the one person whose opinion really mattered or those of his close advisers.

This argument needs, to be sure, some qualifications over and above the point already made, that the courts of Roman Emperors resembled those of Chinese in the crucial respect that in both civili-sations, Emperors had the last word. We may also note that the phenomenon of multiple audiences is relevant to China as much as it is to Greece. If memorials to the throne are specific to the particular occasion on which they are presented, the principles of good govern-ment are general – even if Chinese writers do not tend to insist, as Plato did, that those principles have to be immutable. The Classics, the cosmological Summa such as the *Lüshi chunqiu*, and the dynastic Histories, all deal with recurring patterns of human behaviour. Sima Qian's *Shiji*, for instance, celebrates the past and offers critical comments on the course of events. But he reaches out beyond his contemporary audience (where indeed, as I noted, he ran into trouble with the Emperor Wu Di), and he expresses his hope that his work will prove useful to future generations.

But the thesis may be confirmed, rather than weakened, by some of the evidence of those who might be thought exceptions to the general rule, either because they turned their back on conventional values, or because they lacked access to the seats of power and influence. We saw in Chapter 1 that even those texts that advocate doing nothing, *wu wei*, sometimes turn that into a policy for government. The sage king rules by example, not by intervention. Zhuangzi refused office, but his favourite interlocutor, Hui Shi, was chief minister in the state of Wei. Zhuangzi is represented as bereft of anyone to talk to, once Hui Shi was dead (*Zhuangzi* 24: 48-51) and that may suggest that he still needed an audience the better to elaborate his own position, even if that is very different from the conventional Chinese audience of a ruler in court. Again Liu An, the organiser of *Huainanzi*, which also advocates *wu wei*, was king of Huainan and sent his book to his uncle the Emperor Wu Di, even though he later fell from favour and had to take his own life.

The case of Wang Chong is perhaps especially interesting. I noted before that he failed to advance beyond a very humble position in his official career and this led him to retire as a recluse to write the *Lun Heng*. In it he complained (as Confucius had done) of the lack of a wise ruler to appreciate his talents. But he is exceptional in that he self-consciously argues that he deserves a hearing, even though he does not hold office nor is in a position of influence. He should be listened to, nevertheless, because his book contains valuable advice. His audience is an imaginary one – people who, he hopes, will benefit from his critical and sceptical comments on the mores of the day – but the raison d'être of his work remains strictly analogous to that of the memorials to the throne that he might have presented if he had been well placed at court to do so. Even those who had no chance of an audience with a prince still used the same general criterion of utility to advertise the merits of their work.

The primary rules and conventions that governed speaker/audience, author/readership, interactions in China diverge in certain important respects from those of Greece. Most literary works, in both ancient civilisations, were the products of the literate elite, sometimes of very highly privileged members of it. But Chinese authors were not generally distracted by an idea that weighed with many Greeks (even though it was violently rejected by Plato), namely that the ultimate forum of judgement was a peer group of your fellow citizens. The Assembly in action was a formative experience in real life for many

Greeks of the classical period, and it seems to lie in the background of much Greek literature, including drama, where dialectical confrontations between persons and values are regularly staged both in tragedy and comedy. The nearest we can get to an equivalent dominant frame in China is that of the audience with the king or his ministers, often the primary occasions for both real and imaginary persuasions. To be sure, in technical writing, in astronomy or mathematics or medicine, Chinese specialists mainly had other specialists in mind as the people to contend with. They were certainly not always thinking about what might find favour with the authorities. But the notion of proving your worth, in the final analysis by showing the utility of your ideas for the benefit of 'all under heaven', that idea had greater penetration, or is more pervasive in more genres of literature, in China than it can be said to have ever been in Greece.

*

It is time now to turn to our own situation today, where the conventions of exchange differ strikingly from those of the ancient world across the spectrum of political and intellectual life. Let me concentrate on two particular features, first in the general intellectual, then in the more particular political, domain. First there is what we may call the democratisation of communication, especially via the internet[6] – and secondly there is a certain asymmetry in many communicative exchanges, affecting especially the degree of responsibility and of accountability of the participants.

In academic life, the internet has made it possible to bypass conventional publishers, and publish your work directly. That no more guarantees that it will reach a wide readership than more traditional modes do, but the potential advantages are clear. The publication of a work does not depend on someone else's decision about whether it is commercially, or even intellectually, viable. Traditional publishing houses, including university presses, some of them subsidised, are, meanwhile, under increasing economic pressure, and not just because of the usual cycles of world economic recession. They may be relieved that some specialised studies, from recently completed PhDs, are published directly on the web. But certainly that other recent technological innovation, photocopying, has drastically affected the sales of conventionally produced books. Yet the increase in new titles every year continues, with a corresponding increase in the difficulty of getting them noticed, for example in getting them reviewed even in specialist journals. Nevertheless, on balance, the web is a democratising influence, even though its reach is limited, of course, to those who have access to it.

Going solo on the web, to publish on your own account, has, however, some of the taint of vanity publishing. The more important media, for serious academic work across the spectrum from the humanities and the social sciences to the sciences, are still the technical journals – many of those too, to be sure, now also available on the web. Here for the acceptance of an article, blind peer group review is the norm, and in principle that helps to ensure an unbiased hearing for new ideas. In practice, however, as I said in Chapter 2, such ideas still often have barriers to overcome. Radically innovative work has to make the most of the pluralism of possible outlets to gain a hearing. Even if one avenue of advancement and recognition may be blocked, there are others that can be tried. The conservativism of professors is an inhibitory factor but thankfully often no match for the ambitions of each new generation of students. The word gets around – often again via discussion groups on the net, more rarely, nowadays, through actual personal encounters at colloquia – and although many new fashions turn out to be dead ends, the competitiveness of academic life stimulates innovation.

While as I argued in Lloyd 2004 much remains unsatisfactory in relations between the universities and their political masters, the position of academics now certainly compares favourably in certain respects with Greek or with Chinese antiquity. The former simply failed to provide any regular institutional support for research, while in the latter that support came with strings attached, a closer commitment to the authorities' agenda, and there were severer penalties for non-compliance. We do not now hear of academics being forced by their political masters to take their own lives – even though some do in despair or under pressure, and some may be obliged, or have chosen, to leave their own country.

When we turn now to the management of political communication, however, the situation is very different. First, the problem of multiple audiences is acute. The politician talks to his or her party congress, or addresses Parliament, but what he or she says will be reported on the national and may also be on the international news. That is all to the good, from one point of view, since it makes it rather more difficult for politicians to be, in the famous phrase, 'economical with the truth', saying one thing to one audience, to please or at least not to antagonise them, but adopting a very different tack in other circumstances, when the hard decisions have to be taken.

It is the job of the media to expose such double talk, and to press politicians who try to evade the issues by obfuscation or equivocation. Yet it is at that point that questions to do with the symmetry of responsibility enter in. Politicians have to submit to the verdict of the electorate (those who bother to vote, that is) once every four or five years. Those who cross-examine them for the media are accountable, if at all, only eventually to the proprietors or ruling bodies of their newspapers or television stations – and they are more likely to use audience ratings, than politically responsible behaviour, as their criteria for performance. The media themselves may arrange programmes to assess public opinion on particular issues, even when it is not election time. But there is a big question-mark over the reliability of such polling, and this will in any event happen only when the media bosses themselves find it suits them.

The interactions I have so far spoken of are mediated by the spoken word. Yet as powerful, in many ways more powerful, carriers of messages are the visual images that are a necessary part of all TV programmes. Their ambiguities are different from those of the spoken word. How to interpret what we see is more open-ended than what we hear, and just as liable to manipulation. There are occasional programmes that expose how the images have been selected and edited by the programme producers who used them. In addition to the daily reporting of the Iraq war there were programmes that dealt with how it was reported. But one never gets beyond the decisions of editors even when they decide to discuss other editors.

The images are often repeated many times over in the course of a single programme, especially on world news reports such as those on CNN and the BBC world service. We are expected to take them at face value. We can see, can we not, what happened, sometimes even witnessing it as it happens. There is no gainsaying that the building was bombed, the passer-by injured, the innocent child rushed to hospital. But how were the shots taken? Who sent the reporters in to film at just that place and time, or why were the stringers on hand? In the more predictable events, say at political demonstrations, we may wonder whether the presence of reporters itself acted as a stimulus encouraging the acts filmed, even at the limit provoking them deliberately.

While the horror comes over with devastating effect, that is sometimes all that comes over. The larger picture, and the background to the human tragedies reported, are sometimes sidelined – as the drive continues to find 'breaking news'. In the first major conflict which was reported by TV direct from the battlefield, the Vietnam war, the effect of media coverage was to bring home immediately to a worldwide audience events that would otherwise not have been recorded at all, or only in conventional cabled articles with very limited illustrations. The effect on public opinion in the USA and across the world was dramatic, although the authorities in the States took some time to realise this. Subsequently much stricter controls have been imposed on reporting from war areas at least, though that is certainly difficult in such situations as the Palestine-Israeli conflict. Pictures of the return of US corpses from 'pacified' Iraq were banned, even though Italian casualties were given full State funerals. Yet in some cases, in the reporting of malnutrition for example, the media have often paid less attention to their responsibility for providing full information than to a search for the most horrifying images.

Although the modern world is so much more complex than the ancient, the possibility of being better informed about what happens even in remote or war-torn regions is far greater than it ever was in antiquity. Yet the problems of who to believe, and what to believe, remain, and are, if anything, exacerbated because the manipulators so often work behind the scenes. In the Assemblies and Dicasteries of ancient Greece and in the Imperial Court in China there were, to be sure, plenty of opportunities for misleading, including telling downright lies. Those who listened to the speeches or heard witnesses report distant or even local events, had to use all their canniness and experience to detect fraudsters and they often proved wrong in their judgement. Yet if the audience was taken in it had only itself to blame.

Nowadays we have, with certain exceptions, a much more passive role. We do not usually have a chance to cross-examine those who are responsible for bringing us the news, including those responsible for deciding what to bring. We only rarely have an opportunity to quiz politicians, and that is more likely to be on the internet than face to face at a party congress. We can participate in rallies and demonstrations. Those are *our* chief participatory Assemblies, though they are not ones where we can say that *isêgoria* prevails. But otherwise we merely spectate as the confrontation between the Prime Minister and the Leader of the Opposition is excerpted for us in a more or less narrowly selective version on the radio or TV. The vividness of the images in the latter case gives the illusion of presence: but we are passive spectators, and the images mask the fact that they are always mediated by editors and producers, when not by the politicians themselves. We lack any sense of equality of access to information, such a feature of Greek Assemblies and law-courts and even to a lesser extent among the entourage of Chinese rulers.

Many of the key players on whom we depend for our information are not subject to any regular process of evaluation or scrutiny – not unless they are brought to court and sued for libel or called before an investigating committee set up by Parliament or Congress. In the case of Iraq's purported weapons of mass destruction, criticism of the heads of intelligence agencies for the accuracy of the advice they had given may have served to reprimand them, but was also used in an attempt to exonerate the politicians who took the decision to go to war.

We are used to thinking of modern political institutions as the inheritors of the democratic ideals of Greek antiquity. That can be upheld with regard to two principles especially, that each vote should be counted as equal to every other one, and that those who hold office should be accountable in the sense of subject to re-election. Yet it can hardly be sustained in a third respect, with regard to the contrast between a participatory, and a representative, democracy, between a democracy with an Assembly of the people, and one without. In that respect the modern remoteness of those who rule from those they rule has more in common with the situation in ancient China than that in ancient Greek democracies. That remoteness does not diminish their eventual accountability – when we have a chance to replace our politicians at election time. But where the media are concerned, accountability is still scarcely acknowledged as essential in principle and it is certainly only weakly implemented in practice – and that despite the other great progress that technology has facilitated in what I called the democratisation of communication.

4

The Delusions of Invulnerability

The world's literatures from different periods and in many different languages are full of expressions of the frailty of the human condition. The underlying point is banal, but it can prompt great poetry and be the subject of moving prose. Some react with sadness and resignation. But others resist the implications, deny that there is cause for gloom, suggest ways of snatching victory from the jaws of defeat, present a brave, a confident, even a triumphant front. Can invulnerability somehow be secured, and if so, how?

I shall examine the complex sets of reactions found in four different cultures, pagan ancient Greek, ancient Chinese, early Christian and our own situation. Let me anticipate my argument in summary form.

The pagan ancient Greeks were obsessed by the notion of the vulnerability of humans, whom many represented as the playthings of capricious gods, and they propounded both religious and philosophical antidotes. They expressed belief in different notions of immortality, some more, some less, linked to an ethics and to the idea of rewards and punishments in the afterlife. Different philosophical schools (as we saw) all offered their followers freedom from anxiety, *ataraxia*, but which philosophers was one to believe?

Plenty of ancient Chinese texts speak eloquently of the fluctuations in human prosperity, but the Chinese did not feel threatened by envious gods. The dominant notion of immortality is a physical one, not the immortality of a disembodied soul. The cycles of *yin* and *yang*, and the constancy of change, are accepted with equanimity. It would be absurd to fight against them. The *dao* is not a matter of intellectual certainty, but an ideal one should strive to embody. The goal was not the strictly impossible one of invulnerability, but the admittedly difficult one of sagehood.

The Christian solution gave a new twist to pagan notions of a personal immortality where good was rewarded and evil punished. Justice was now dispensed by a single all-powerful god. What happens to you in this life is of no consequence compared with the fate of your immortal soul in the next. The invulnerability of eternal salvation was mirrored by the inescapability of eternal damnation. But the salvation in question was in any case exclusive to Christians: limbo was the best that most pagans could hope for.

Finally, the yearning for invulnerability has certainly come back to haunt us with a vengeance today. But this is now associated with a quite different set of dominant values, not those of the ancient pagan Greeks intent on glory and honour, nor those of the Chinese who focused on virtues and the welfare of 'all under heaven', nor yet those of the Christian ideal of charity. Rather, they are the values of egotism and materialism. The paradox is that the more the immediate problems of subsistence become – for some – irrelevant, the greater the sense of other threats to the prosperity thus attained, threats not just from those who have not had the good fortune to attain it – the have-nots – but also from those who disagree fundamentally with those Western values. But inward-looking, self-regarding solutions – the increasing fortification of prosperous communities and whole states, of fortress America especially – can be no more than stop-gaps and may, in certain circumstances, even exacerbate the situation. Security – the other cultures we shall examine confirm – can never be a matter just of externals. The problems are certainly now global and the solutions must be too: at the very least they depend, so I shall argue, on a recovery of a sense of collective solidarity.

*

Greek literature, from its very outset, presents some of the most poignant expressions of human frailty. The generations of men are like those of leaves, scattered by the wind, as the famous simile at *Iliad* 6 146ff. puts it, a theme echoed and elaborated by Mimnermus, Simonides and many others. 'We are like leaves that many-flowered springtime bears', says Mimnermus (2) 'which grow quickly in the light of the sun. Like them we enjoy the flower of youth for just a season, knowing from the gods neither good nor evil. But the black fates stand by, one holding the goal of bitter old age, the other that of death. The fruit of youth is shortlived – like the time it takes the sun to spread over the earth. But when once that season of perfection is past, then indeed to die would be better than to live.'

The shortness of human life, the transitoriness of youth and the bitterness of old age, are topics taken up by one lyric poet after another. Semonides (1) adds the delusions of hope. 'There is no wit (*noös*) in humans. We live each day as it comes, like cattle, knowing nothing of how the god will bring each one to its end. Hope and trust nourish all of us as we strive for the unattainable.' But what we encounter are premature old age, disease, death in war or shipwreck, or suicide. 'Thus nothing is without evil. Yes, ten thousand dooms, woes and unthought-of griefs are the lot of mankind.' Simonides quotes the *Iliad* passage (eleg. 8) and says that people ignore its lessons, and elsewhere expostulates (520): 'As for humans, small is their strength, fruitless their cares, brief their life, toil upon toil.' Inescapable death hangs over everyone, good and bad alike. 'God is all-devising: for mortals, nothing is free from evil' (526).

For this awful state of affairs, the archaic didactic poet Hesiod has an explanation in the form of the myth of Prometheus and the creation of the first woman, Pandora. Prometheus steals fire from Zeus and gives it to humans. But in revenge (*Works* 70ff.) Zeus causes Hephaestus to make Pandora, who is endowed with skills by Athena and with beauty by Aphrodite. Prometheus' brother Epimetheus foolishly accepts the gift of Pandora, with disastrous results. Before Pandora (90ff.) the tribes of humans had lived on earth without ills, without hard work, without terrible diseases. But Pandora lifts the lid of the jar in which the gods' gifts are stored, and all these evils escape. 'The earth is full of evils, and the sea is full' (101).

The helplessness of humans is pointed up, time and again, by way of contrast with the power of the gods, not just the supreme god, Zeus, but the whole pantheon of the Olympians and the Chthonians (the gods of the underworld). In the *Iliad* some gods favour one side, others the other, and the ebb and flow of battle reflects a complex combination of the prowess of human heroes and the varying and conflicting manipulations of their divine supporters. In one picaresque scene in *Iliad* 5 311ff. the Greek warrior Diomedes even takes on Aphrodite, who has intervened to protect her son Aeneas. He wounds the goddess, drawing not blood, but *ichor* (340), but while that causes her to retreat and seek consolation from her mother Dione on Olympus, back on the battlefield Apollo stops Diomedes with a reminder not to think he can match the gods – since 'in no way similar is the tribe of the immortal gods to that of humans who go upon the ground' (440ff.).

Greek polytheism dictated that there was more than one divinity to whom you might turn for help. But by the same argument there was more than one who might be out to harm you. True, the rights and wrongs of their quarrels are ultimately decided by Zeus (cf. Lloyd-Jones 1983), but not even he is in total control in the short term – as his being distracted by Hera's elaborate seduction in *Iliad* 14 shows. Odysseus has Athena on his side throughout the *Odyssey*, but many of the tribulations he faces on his long voyage home are the work of Poseidon. In tragedy it is Hippolytus who illustrates the double-bind humans face most vividly. His devotion to Artemis leads him to dishonour Aphrodite who announces in the prologue of Euripides' play that she will have her revenge (21f.) and duly does.

Further misfortunes may threaten not because of what you do, but because of what your ancestors did. If your own actions, ignoring some advice from the gods, some prophecy, for instance, do not get you into trouble, the deeds of your forefathers may and the whole family to which you belong may be cursed for generations. Again there is a complex balance between what humans bring upon themselves (whether or not they could, in some sense, have acted otherwise) and what the gods are directly responsible for. Oedipus himself lays a curse on his two sons, Polyneices and Eteocles – though it takes more than just his cursing them for them to kill one another. But further back in Oedipus' family his own father Laius had disobeyed Apollo's warning in having a child. He had been cursed by Pelops who was himself cursed by his father-in-law

Oenomaus for cheating in the way he won Oenomaus' daughter Hippodamia as his bride. Human agents are at work at every step, but the whole story of the accursedness of the lineage starts with Tantalus, who offended the gods by serving up his son Pelops in a dish at a feast for them.

Heracles' misfortunes stem more directly from the vindictiveness of Hera. First she attempted to obstruct his birth (his mother Alcmene had been made pregnant both by a mortal, Amphitryon, and by Zeus: that is what upset Hera) and delayed it so that not he but Eurystheus should become king of Argos. Then she sent snakes to attack him in his cradle, though the infant Heracles strangled them. Worst of all, she made him mad so that he killed his own wife and sons – for which he is punished by having to serve Eurystheus who imposes the famous twelve Labours on him – though in the version in Euripides' *Heracles* the Labours precede, rather than follow, his being made mad.

Hera's persecution of Heracles is exceptional. But the general theme of the gods' *phthonos* – envy or malice – towards humans is common. It is emphatically denied, twice, by Plato, *Phaedrus* 247a and *Timaeus* 29e, and Plato would not have needed to do that unless the idea was still being taken seriously in his day. However, when Aristotle contradicts it in his turn, *Metaphysics* 982b32-983a6, he says it is 'what poets say' and 'poets often lie'. Yet outside poetry, where it is found in epic, lyric and tragedy,[1] it appears repeatedly in, for example, Herodotus. Solon, famous for his wisdom, is made to tell Croesus that *to theion* – the divine, the godhead (he names no names) – is full of envy (*phthoneros*) and trouble (I 32). Herodotus seems to endorse the point himself in his comment at I 34 that after Solon's visit, a great retribution, *nemesis*, came on Croesus from god, 'as it seems' (*hôs eikasai*) because he thought himself the most blessed of all humans. In the story of Polycrates it is the Egyptian king Amasis who warns him in similar terms, when he says that he cannot take pleasure in Polycrates' great good fortune, since he knows 'the divine' is envious (III 40), and at VII 46 it is Artabanus' turn to call god envious when he and his nephew Xerxes exchange views on the shortness of human life and the troubles and diseases that afflict it.[2]

On a number of occasions writers in different genres put the blame for human misery firmly on humans themselves and represent a just god as rewarding the good and punishing the wicked. Hesiod's *Works* (225ff.) claims that the city ruled by just kings prospers, enjoys peace and is free from famine and disaster (*atê*, ruin, and especially the delusion that leads to it). As for the evil city, that gets punished by Zeus with famine, plague and infertility. The manner in which arrogance, *hubris*, gets its just deserts is the mainspring of many a tragedy. But again the theme is to be found also in prose. The way in which the excesses of barbarian rulers are punished by their downfall is a recurrent topic in Herodotus. He remarks, for instance, with regard to the Lydian king Candaules already at I 8 that he inevitably found misfortune because of his infatuation with his own wife's beauty. He gets Gyges to spy on her naked, but she discovers him and forthwith offers him the choice of killing her husband or being put to death himself. At II 111 Pheros son of Sesostris is blinded for having hurled a spear at the Nile when it flooded excessively. Elsewhere, however, Herodotus hedges his bets. In the story of the Persian king Cambyses' crazy decision to kill the bull sacred to Apis, at III 28ff., Herodotus reports, as one possibility, that Cambyses was simply a sufferer from the sacred disease: but he also records the Egyptians' view that Cambyses' subsequent madness was the direct result of his sacrilege.

But in Herodotus it is not just barbarian excess and arrogance that are punished. At IV 202ff. he tells the story of Pheretime who had taken vengeance on the people of Barce for Arcesilaus' death by impaling the men, cutting off the breasts of the women and putting them on stakes round the city wall. But she goes on to die a gruesome death, her body eaten alive by worms, which elicits Herodotus' comment that 'excessive retribution exacted by humans is hateful in the eyes of the gods' (205). Then in his complex handling of the madness of Cleomenes, king of Sparta, Herodotus again hedges his bets. He reports the Spartans' own view that the problem arose from Cleomenes drinking his wine neat – a habit he had picked up from associating with Scythians. But he also records several other explanations, in each of which Cleomenes' madness is seen as divine retribution for some act of sacrilege he had committed. One version is that he had suborned the Pythian priestess to deny that Demaratus was the son of Ariston, which led to Demaratus being deposed (VI 65ff.), and Herodotus comes close to endorsing this. For him (84) Cleomenes' madness was a punishment for 'what he had done to Demaratus'.

While some classical Greek texts develop the idea that Zeus is there to secure justice and distribute rewards and punishments to the good and wicked respectively, others recognise that it is not just the latter who suffer misfortune. Of course for those who were inclined towards theodicy, if someone had suffered some calamity, the temptation was to try to identify what either he or his ancestors had done to deserve this. But just as often (maybe more often) the frailty of human existence and the fickleness of fortune are expressed without the accompanying moralising gloss – to the effect that we can avoid calamity if we behave ourselves and keep on the right side of the supreme dispenser of justice, Zeus.

One common theme that serves to underline human vulnerability is that no one can be accounted *eudaimôn*, 'happy', until they are dead. It is important to note that *eudaimôn* and *eudaimonia* do not refer (as English 'happy' and 'happiness' often do) to transient states, a feeling of joyfulness or contentment. Rather, they relate to the whole tenor of a person's life. When Aristotle discusses the dictum, as he does both in *Nicomachean Ethics* 1100a10ff. and in *Eudemian Ethics* 1219b1ff., he associates it especially with Solon, as does Herodotus (I 32, using the expression *olbios*, 'blessed/prosperous', when he represents Solon in conversation with Croesus: and cf. Solon himself in poem 13). While Aristotle recognises the paradoxicality of the saying, insofar as 'happiness' is an activity, and so the dead cannot be said to be happy, he allows that Solon was right in saying that judgement about a person's *eudaimonia* is premature until his or her end is known.[3] It says a great deal about the Greek sense of human vulnerability that even Aristotle, confident as he is in his own moral philosophy, endorses the dictum on that point. It is as if most Greeks, much of the time, expected that misfortune might strike at any moment.

But if, as seems to be the case, the ancient Greeks had a heightened sense of the potential for misery that goes with the human condition, we may ask what resources they could call on to alleviate the situation. We saw that Mimnermus put it bluntly that rather than face old age it is better to die. There are indeed many cases where, if dishonour threatens, a person takes his own life, both in literature (as in the case of Ajax in Sophocles' play) and in actuality (where the Stoic Seneca followed the precepts of his own philosophy in committing suicide – though of course he was forced by Nero to do so).

For the Homeric hero, the main values that made life worth living were honour (*timê*), glory (*kudos*) and fame (*kleos*). In the *Iliad* Achilles knows he is doomed to die young, but prefers a glorious but short life, to a comparatively inglorious old age. Poetry itself, the poets keep reminding us, keeps alive the memory of great deeds (a claim echoed in prose by Herodotus when he tells us why he wrote his *Histories* I 1). However, Achilles' choice is put into perspective in the *Odyssey*. When interviewed by Odysseus in the underworld (*Odyssey* 11 471ff.) he rebuts Odysseus' suggestion that no man was ever more blessed than himself nor ever will be, with the statement: 'do not comfort me with respect to death'. He would prefer to serve as a hired man to a poor man on earth rather than rule over all the corpses of the dead.

Yet two main lines of thought came to be developed that offered those who accepted them a way of compensating for, or withstanding, the miseries of human life. The first is a belief in immortality in some of its versions, the second that with philosophy you can secure true happiness, indeed become immune to anxiety.

The belief in immortality takes many different forms in ancient Greece. There is a shadowy existence after death, as we have just seen, in Homer. Among more substantial representations of the possibilities of the afterlife, some put the emphasis on purity, some on morality, some on both. When morality was in question, the prospects of being judged on your life could strike terror as much as they could offer hope – depending on how you had spent your life. In the mystery religions, ritual initiation was the key to salvation. But in the Pythagorean belief in the transmigration of souls, for which our best early evidence comes in Empedocles, what happens to you in your next incarnation certainly reflects how you have behaved in this one. There is a hierarchy of more, and less, noble beings, among humans, among other animals and plants, and the *daimôn* might move up or down, in its next incarnation, both within those orders and between them. However, the ultimate aim was certainly not personal immortality, but rather to escape the cycle of rebirth, the *kuklos barupenthês*, altogether. While that cycle continued, the outlook was grim.

Quite what form of immortality Plato believed in is at points unclear, for some texts suggest that reason alone survives (*Timaeus* 69c ff.), while others seem to imply that the soul as a whole may (*Phaedrus*). What identifies Socrates' soul as Socrates' in its disembodied state? There are difficulties in squaring the doctrines of the soul proposed in different dialogues (*Phaedo*, *Gorgias* and *Republic* especially), and in reconciling the vivid images presented in the eschatological myths with the formal analyses to which they are usually the coda. But on several fundamental points there is no room for doubt.

First, Plato is convinced that the universe is the work of a benevolent god: indeed his creation is the fairest and the best of living creatures, as the end of the *Timaeus* (92c) puts it. Secondly, each person is responsible for his or her own life. No one does wrong willingly, but rather out of ignorance. Wrong-doing harms your soul, and once you realise that, you will of course avoid it. Your responsibility extends indeed beyond this life, for it is the key factor that determines the future destiny of your immortal soul. The end of the *Republic* (614b ff.) presents this in mythical terms. Souls are judged according to how they have lived. When it comes to their being reborn, they draw lots to determine the order in which they make their choice among the next lives they are to lead. Odysseus is said by chance to have drawn the last lot of all, and he chooses the quiet life of a private citizen. But he says he would have chosen it even if he had been first in the lottery (620cd). Whatever we make of the detail of that scene, it is emphatically stated that the responsibility for the choice lies with the chooser, and that god himself is blameless (*anaitios*) (617e).

The greater the emphasis on your personal responsibility for your life, the more demanding the Platonic ethic can be seen to be. But with a benevolent god in control, you can be sure at least of ultimate cosmic justice. Socrates may have been wrongly convicted by the Athenians, but he faces the death penalty with equanimity, confident that he has done no wrong and that he has served the Athenian people well by constantly challenging their beliefs.

Aristotle shares much of Plato's idealism about the joys of reason and the superiority of the philosophical to all other lives. But the belief in personal immortality is not one he endorses. Granted that (unlike the gods) we cannot philosophise continually, we can and should practise the moral and political virtues, courage, justice, generosity and so on. They in turn depend, up to a point, on external goods, birth, wealth and health, and the first, and to some extent the second and third, are beyond the philosopher's control.

For both Plato and Aristotle the philosopher is resolute in the face of apparent misfortune, confident in his or her *aretê*. Yet neither guaranteed total immunity from troubles, care or anxiety. But it was just this that the major Hellenistic philosophical schools claimed to deliver, even though they differed, as I noted before, both on what *ataraxia* consisted in and on how to go about achieving it.

Both Epicureans and Stoics subordinated 'logic' and 'physics' to 'ethics': the first two studies are undertaken for the sake of the third. You needed 'physics', the Epicureans thought, to give you the correct doctrines on fundamental reality – atoms and the void – and to rid yourself of superstitious beliefs, such as that the gods are responsible for natural phenomena. There are gods, they still thought – the images that come to us, in dreams for example, show that – and although quite what form they take is controversial,[4] it is clear the Epicureans held that they have no concern for this or any other world. As for such phenomena as lightning and thunder and earthquakes, the job of the physicist is to show that they have natural causes. In such cases the Epicureans did not think it sensible to assign a single cause for each phenomenon. If, as was usually the case, several could be suggested as possible (on the basis of analogy, for instance), all should be kept in play. The aim was to establish that *some* natural cause is at work. The Epicureans were well aware that the gods had generally been assumed to be active agents in the world, and the efforts they devoted to countering this belief testify to the hold it continued to have, both in the fourth century BCE and later.

The correct views on ethics were even more important. The good was equated with the pleasant, but choosing that, in any given context, involved a careful calculation balancing present pleasures and pains with future ones, and more stable with more transient ones. The soul is corporeal – it consists of atoms – but a distinction could still be drawn between mental and purely physical pleasures and pains. Even in the face of physical pain, brought about by disease, the sage would be happy, reminding himself or herself of the joys of friendship, the pleasure of past philosophical conversations and the like. So the sage would be happy, *eudaimôn*, even under torture on the rack (Diogenes Laertius X 118). The claim was that this whole philosophy gave you freedom from anxiety that *nothing*, no seeming misfortune, could shake.

The Stoics too got to the same conclusion – of the imperturbability of the sage even under torture – but did so via a different route. Not only were their physics and cosmology different, based on the continuum, not on atoms and the void, but so too especially was their ethics. The good is identified with virtue. Most of the things that were normally prized as goods – beauty, wealth, life itself – are indifferent (neither good nor bad) though some are 'preferred' indifferents. The only real good is virtue – and this is under the control of the individual person. It is up to each one of us to cultivate and practise virtue. Faced with an intolerable situation, the sage would take his or her own life, but that would not be bad, for the only true evil is vice. Secure in their virtue, the sages enjoyed peace of mind – though the Stoics conceded that sagehood was difficult to achieve and the examples of actual sages were limited to Socrates and some legendary figures such as Heracles.

The third approach, Scepticism, took different forms in the hands of different teachers,[5] but we may use Sextus Empiricus as a primary source for what passed as Pyrrhonism in his day, in the second century CE. On every question to do with underlying reality

97

and hidden causes the correct attitude was not to plump for one or other positive, dogmatist, solution – whether the Epicurean, the Stoic, the Aristotelian or whatever – but to suspend judgement. The Sceptics observed the disagreements between those different schools – on whether the cosmos is eternal or created, whether there is just one cosmos or many, whether the physical elements, time and space are all continua or consist of indivisibles – and they exploited them to undermine every positive position. For every argument on one side of such disputes another could be suggested against it: this is the principle of *isostheneia*, 'equal strength', that I have mentioned before.

Suspending judgement, the Sceptic lived by the appearances alone. Yet that suspension of judgement, *epochê*, had precisely the same effect as positive solutions did for the Stoics and Epicureans, namely it secured *ataraxia*. Realising that there was just as much to be said on one side of disputed issues as on the other brought the Sceptics peace of mind. They did not set out with that as the goal of their inquiry; rather it supervened on their inquiring. They told the story of the painter Apelles to illustrate this. Trying to convey the foam on a horse's mouth in a painting, but being unable to do so, he threw his brush at the work, only to find that it created precisely the effect he had been looking for.

So all three major Hellenistic philosophical schools offered invulnerability to fortune – an invulnerability that came, in two cases, from the discovery of the correct answers to the problems of life, and in the third from the realisation that there were no positive answers there to be had. All these philosophers were keen to provide the freedom from anxiety that they all saw as the key to happiness. There was, however, the obvious problem, for those who were not already convinced that one or other school was right, namely *which* to choose to follow. They could not all be right. Even the Sceptics, with their argument that there was no positive theory to be had, might be mistaken. Besides, you might agree with that Sceptic argument and still not see it as securing happiness.

None of the three philosophical schools I have been discussing had any great interest in promoting detailed empirical investigations into the material world. Both Epicureans and Stoics thought that it was important to grasp the fundamental principles of physics – on which, as I have pointed out, they differed profoundly – but with very few exceptions among the Stoics,[6] and none among the Epicureans, they did not engage in the type of research in astronomy, optics, harmonics, geography and medicine that some of their contemporaries were undertaking. Sustained attempts were made by the Greeks, from Eudoxus onwards, to provide adequate models to account for the movements of the sun, moon and planets. The aim was to give geometrical models which would explain the apparent irregularities in the movements and allow them ultimately to be predicted. Yet the successive attempts made never succeeded in resolving all the problems.

In the second century CE, Ptolemy produced a sophisticated combination of epicycles and eccentrics that proved remarkably accurate (by the standards of the day) in accounting for the longitudinal movements of the sun, moon and planets. But in book XIII ch. 2 of the *Syntaxis* he recognises the problems he had especially in dealing with the movements of the planets in latitude – that is, north and south of the ecliptic. He anticipates that his hypotheses will be thought 'troublesome', yet he pleads they are the simplest that can be suggested. The heavenly bodies are unchanging, and it is assumed that their motions are regular, simple and indeed effortless. That belief remains unshaken, despite the apparent complexity of the models that are the best he can propose to explain the phenomena.

It was all very well, some people might have felt, for the Stoics and Epicureans to say that they could guarantee your peace of mind. But how could you rest content when you were surrounded by large numbers of phenomena whose causes were not at all, or barely, understood? In time, the early Christians were to make much of the apparent impasse that pagan natural philosophy had reached in many areas. They considered the situation scandalous and a sure sign that pagan ambitions were misplaced. You do not need curiosity, Tertullian famously protested, when you have Jesus Christ. There is no need for research when you have the gospel. But pagans too registered the impasse. Thus Proclus in the fifth century CE laments the lack of an account of the causes of the planes and distances of the planets, 'I mean the true causes, such that when the soul saw them especially it might cease all its travail' (*Outlines of the Astronomical Hypotheses* 238.13ff.).

The shortfall in the accounts available for a wide range of phenomena is all the more apparent in that the Greeks had – as I have noted before – an ambitious model for rigorous demonstrative explanation. It was Aristotle's claim, or at least hope, that the strict mode of axiomatic-deductive demonstration he defines and illustrates in the *Posterior Analytics* should be applicable not just in mathematics but also in 'physics', including the study of living things as well as astronomy and meteorology. Yet the recurrent problem in applying it was in identifying the self-evident indemonstrable axioms from which demonstration was to proceed. Even in mathematics, some of those used, such as Euclid's parallel postulate, were controversial already in antiquity, for some suggested that that should not be an axiom, but a theorem to be proved. As for the application of that style of reasoning in other fields, the difficulties grew the further from pure mathematics one went. The idealisations of Archimedes' statics and hydrostatics were one thing: Galen's ambition to turn parts of medicine into an axiomatic-deductive system seems hopelessly misplaced.[7]

The chorus of Greek voices all offering freedom from anxiety testifies to a deep-seated preoccupation with the issue. But to ordinary people the philosophers' arguments seemed to undermine one another, and in practice few of the scientists delivered secure causal explanations of the type that some of them, too, demanded. Some of the simpler, cruder, anthropomorphic ideas of the gods had been rebutted by rational criticism, though that did not seriously affect the city-state religion or the cults of the major divinities. In one way, indeed, insecurity itself became an object of worship. From the fourth century BCE onwards, the cult of *Tuchê*, chance, became increasingly widespread across the Greco-Roman world. Caprice thus came to be recognised as fundamental to the human condition. You could not negate the effects of chance: so you turned it into a deity to whom you prayed. In that sense, the eventual pagan Greek 'solution' to the problem of human frailty was to give it official recognition with a cult of its own.

*

The question that I now wish to raise is the following. How far are the ideas and beliefs we have sketched out distinctive of ancient Greek preoccupations, and how far do they reflect concerns that can be paralleled elsewhere? What can a cross-cultural study of the modalities of the expressions of human vulnerability – and of how to respond to it – tell us about the values of the cultures or societies in question, and what light does that throw on the situation in which we find ourselves today? My next case-study is ancient Chinese thought, where I shall concentrate, as usual, on the period down to the end of the Han, that is say before Buddhism became a major influence. Even in the ancient period the Chinese materials we can consider are as diverse as those we have surveyed for ancient Greece.

At first sight many Chinese intuitions of human vulnerability, and many responses to it, appear similar to those we have discussed from pagan Greek antiquity. The cycles of good and bad fortune, and the idea that prosperity does not endure, are common Chinese motifs in poetry and in prose. Many exemplary tales in such texts as *Zhanguoce* and *Huainanzi* follow the sequence of apparent success, leading to self-indulgence and arrogance, leading in turn to disaster. In some, though not all cases, the root causes of human downfall are traced to the faults of the proud themselves.[8] It is a common theme in early Chinese medicine that diseases often come from the excesses of self-indulgence.[9]

As for securing invulnerability, two Chinese themes again at first sight seem broadly similar to Greek ones. Immortality provided one great source of hope: elaborate practices of self-cultivation were developed to achieve it and much effort expended by, and on behalf of, Emperors and others, to obtain drugs and elixirs that could produce the desired result. Secondly, Chinese philosophy, like Greek, offers consolation. The sage's virtue, we are told in the *Lunyu*, is a protection against disappointment, for example at being spurned and not given a chance to show how good government is to be achieved and the welfare of 'all under heaven' secured.[10]

But in each case there are revealing differences that reflect different values to which we must pay attention. The first question concerning immortality arises precisely in relation to what mode of 'immortality' was the goal. Self-cultivation and the taking of drugs might be thought to offer rather different routes to different ends, and certainly self-cultivation took many different forms. Yet they were combined, in Chinese 'alchemy', as Sivin (1968) especially has shown, in a bid to promote longevity. The hope there was to secure not a blissful existence of a disembodied soul or pure reason, but rather the continuation of physical life, the only kind the Chinese prized, to imitate the supernatural beings called the immortals (*xian*) in being indifferent to age.

There is no classical Chinese parallel to the stark dualism of Platonic psychology, where soul and body are of different ontological status, the one incorporeal, the other not. No more do the ideas of systematic rewards and punishments in the afterlife, and of the reincarnation of the soul in higher or lower forms of being, figure prominently before the influence of Buddhism began to be felt. In classical Chinese thought there are various notions of 'ghosts' (*gui*), 'spirits' (*shen*: the term is also used of gods) and of spiritual aspects of human beings (*hun, po*, sometimes combined in the binome *hunpo*).[11] But none of these is exactly a source of anticipated immortal bliss. Chinese representations of what we may think of as 'paradise' are, in any event, terrestrial, located in islands far to the East or in the realm of the Queen Mother of the West. As for *hunpo*, for instance, that is a subject of concern, even anxiety, since the living should make sure they treat the dead properly and pay them the respect due to them. Illumination (*shenming*), spirituality in that sense, is much to be desired, but that is an ambition for living sagehood and does not lead to any notion that life should be treated as a training for death (as in the Greek *meletê thanatou*).

As for philosophical invulnerability, that too took different forms. As we have discussed before, there were those for whom the way to achieve the *dao* was via inaction, *wu wei*. But that corresponds

neither to the dogmatist Epicurean and Stoic recipes, which identified the good with pleasure and with virtue respectively, nor to the
Greek Sceptic position, where freedom from anxiety supervenes upon
the realisation that no dogmatic position is tenable. Texts that advocate *wu wei*, such as the *Zhuangzi* for instance, do indeed value
freedom from care. There are stories of Zhuangzi himself showing a
lack of concern even at personal bereavement.[12] But that equanimity
does not come from, nor does it presuppose, inquiry: rather, it turns
its back on it. The Greek dogmatist has to inquire to ensure that he
or she has grasped the fundamental principles of reality: the Greek
Sceptic needs to explore all avenues if only to see that they lead
nowhere. Zhuangzi does not even start out on any such path.

But maybe the most profound difference between Greek and
Chinese attitudes relates to the way in which the vagaries of fortune
are thematised. In both ancient civilisations, as I noted, we find
frequent expressions of the inconstancy of human existence, of the
cycles of prosperity and misfortune and the like. Both use such observations as the basis for moralising judgements to the effect that pride
comes before a fall, that self-indulgence should be avoided, and that
the seemingly successful should beware of a change of fortune. But
whereas many Greeks saw themselves as the playthings of the gods
– of the capricious ones of the Homeric pantheon or of Caprice or
Chance itself – the Chinese do not imagine themselves surrounded by
gods making human vulnerability inescapable. The Chinese certainly
have exemplary figures, heroes and heroines in that sense – and anti-
heroes and anti-heroines too – whose stories are used to encourage or
deter. The great sage kings, of the Chinese Golden Age, Yao, Shun
and Yu, have their tyrannical counterparts, Jie and Zhou. In cosmological or cosmogonical accounts Gong Gong crashes into one of the
pillars of heaven and tilts the earth towards the south-east. Yet the
Chinese did not think of themselves as caught between Aphrodite
and Artemis – between sexuality and celibacy – like Hippolytus, or
between Poseidon and Athena, like Odysseus, or faced with an
envious Hera capable of inflicting madness on Heracles. In short,
there was no divine *phthonos* to contend with.[13]

Of course there is no uniformity in Chinese thought on many

fundamental issues, even in the pre-Buddhist period, any more than there is in Greek, and so generalisation is hazardous and always subject to qualifications. As we shall be considering in detail later,[14] Chinese thinkers disagreed on whether humans are inherently good, inherently bad, or neither, and further on where the chief human obligations lie. In the Mohist view, the proper attitude is one of concern for all humans uniformly, to which the Confucians responded by insisting on differentiated hierarchies of obligations. When we come to the all-important matter of securing good government (cf. Chapter 1), the so-called Legalists put the emphasis on law and regulation and penalties and punishments, while others thought that what was needed was for humans to see the importance of virtue and to internalise that themselves.

But over one range of issues there is considerable unanimity of opinion. This concerns the fact of change itself. Change is the most prominent feature not just of human life, but of the cosmos itself. The seasons alternate, the positions of the stars change, cycles of birth, maturity and death govern all living things. This is not just the fundamental message of the *Yijing*, the *Book of Changes*: it is a theme taken up in different forms by most Chinese writers in most genres. Everything is subject to the alternation of *yin* and *yang*. At the very point in the cycle when *yang* is at its strongest, *yin* begins to increase, and conversely the moment of maximum *yin* is when *yang* starts once again to make its presence felt.

Immunity to that kind of change is never contemplated. The sage is the person who adapts to that, shifting with the ever-shifting situation itself. Although different authors certainly offer different recommendations for human behaviour, no attempt is made to deny the fundamental fact of change. We do not find Chinese philosophers bewailing that fact: no more do we find them expressing disgust at the ugliness of old age or proclaiming, in the way that Mimnermus did, that once youth is past it is better to die. To the contrary, for the Chinese once youth was over, you were only just getting into your stride. Where many Greeks privileged the unchanging in many different contexts – the heavenly bodies are unchanging, the truths the philosopher contemplates are eternal ones – the Chinese ideal tends rather to be, not what is immune to change (rest indeed is often associated with stagnation), but one of harmonious interaction. The sage who embodies the *dao* is in tune with the cosmos.

*

There is much more to the variety of Chinese thought down to the end of the Han than I have been able to indicate, and if space permitted, a further complex account of the interaction of new and old responses to human vulnerability could be given in relation to later Chinese thought, once Buddhism came to be a powerful influence, with its doctrine of the need to escape what binds you to the illusory nature of existence. However, as a preparation for a discussion of where we are today, I shall concentrate now, in a brief interlude, on what happened in the West, when it was taken over by that other world religion, Christianity. What difference did that make to the pagan Greek inheritance?

Pagan Greek ideas were, to be sure, only one source among many for early Christian belief: the Judaic influence with regard to the themes I have been discussing is certainly as important, probably more so. But if we compare early Christian with pagan Greek attitudes, some five points stand out as fundamental.

The first vital point is that Christianity does not depend on argument – as Greek philosophy did – but on faith and relevation, on sacred texts and the authority of the Church. Some elements can be paralleled in the pagan mystery religions: but their combination in Christianity is exceptional. The point has added relevance since the 1870 Vatican Council definition of papal infallibility. That often misunderstood doctrine was thereby linked explicitly to statements by the Pope speaking ex cathedra. However, this represents a mode of invulnerability – to error – for which there is no analogue in either pagan Greece or China.

Next, Christian monotheism, like Judaic, differed not only, obviously, from pagan polytheism, but also from Plato's idea of a supreme god. True, Plato's Craftsman is called the father of the universe, though Plato insists that he is difficult to describe and impossible to communicate to others (*Timaeus* 28c, cf. 47b); Plato's contemporaries would have appreciated the profound differences from, as well as the links to, Zeus the father. But the Christian God the Father has far stronger anthropomorphic features than Plato's Craftsman, and of course in his manifestation as God the Son became human. The prospect, for the faithful, of salvation comes with a stronger guarantee than was ever available in Greek mystery religions, for Christ had intervened personally on earth.

Thirdly, what we need saving from is answered in a way that again has no pagan Greek antecedent, namely Original Sin. If the salvation is the more secure, thanks to God the Son, the need for it is all the greater, in that humans otherwise still carry the burden that comes from the Fall. The magnitude of the joy for the forgiveness of sins is proportional to the magnitude of the gloom concerning the sins that are there to be forgiven.

Fourthly, while there is a further point of similarity in that some pagan Greeks had, as we saw, already developed certain notions of the rewards and punishments that human souls are liable to, when judged after death, that set of ideas takes on an altogether more formidable resonance in Christianity. Here there is no sense of the soul being judged through successive incarnations, able to do better, or worse, in successive lives and indeed successive life forms. You have, in Christianity, just the one chance, as it were, and the Last Judgement is just that (and of course animals do not enter into the frame since they do not have immortal souls). Moreover the whole scenario, with not just Paradise for the eternally saved, and Hell for the eternally damned, but Purgatory to cleanse souls of venial sins, is worked out in far greater detail than in any pagan account. In particular, the damnation of the damned in Christian representations of Hell makes the punishments of Sisyphus and Tantalus seem like kindergarten stuff. The Christian God is supposed not to be vindictive in the way the God of the Old Testament often seemed to be: but if mercy is one of his attributes, he certainly still exacts severe penalties for sin.

Finally, there is a further essential point of contrast – where again the Judaic influence is apparent in Christianity – namely that salvation is exclusive to Christians. Eternal bliss in paradise in a sense depends, in the first instance, on an accident of birth, on when you were born, for if you had the misfortune to be born before Christ there was no way in which you could follow him. The most that pre-Christian pagans of any race could hope for was an afterlife in limbo. In Calvinism, salvation further depended upon having been chosen. But the general point is obvious, namely that faith and observance are a *sine qua non* for the kind of invulnerability – to secure eternal life – that Christianity offered.

*

Let me now use this rapid and selective survey of earlier ideas in different cultures as a framework for some reflections on the modern world. The most powerful nation on earth is also one of the youngest, in terms of when it achieved nationhood. The culture of the USA is an amalgam. The original indigenous populations, when not totally exterminated, have been largely confined to reservations. Their pasts provide no great historical depth to today's America. Culturally they are ignored, although that is not the case with those who commandeered their territories, the pioneers who took over their lands and made them their own – as if there were nothing the other side of the frontier they were pushing back. They, the frontiersmen, certainly entered the imagination as models of resourcefulness, independence and self-reliance.

Again, although the modern population of the USA is, in origin, from all parts of the world, the rich histories of those original cultures do not make much impact on America as such, only on some of its constituent parts. True, the War of Independence, the Civil War, later involvements in two World Wars, Korea, Vietnam – all of those go to make up *American* history. But even the most traumatic of those events have done little to affect the sense that the USA is totally unlike any other nation there has ever been, not just in being – undeniably – more powerful than any previous state in history, but also in being especially blessed. Americans are not only not surrounded by envious gods: they are under the protection of a god who surely answers positively every time he is called upon – by those of very different religious beliefs or even of none – to respond to the prayer 'God bless America'.

There have been chosen people before – as my remarks on early Christianity and its Judaic inheritance acknowledged. The difference this time is in what has happened to the rest of the world – and the problem for any chosen people is that there is always a rest of the world. What marks out America is not a matter of race, nor yet of religion (despite my remarks about 'God bless America'), but rather of success and prosperity. But the former is judged by comparison with the rest of the world, the latter in a sense depends on it – since the wealth of America comes in large measure from its dominant position in the world economy.

Yet being the sole super-power on earth does not secure immunity to attack. What was so shocking about September 11 2001 was not the scale of the damage and loss of life – far smaller than that suffered by Hiroshima or Nagasaki, or by many devastated European cities in the Second World War – but rather that it came from an enemy who was in no position to declare war, and it happened on American soil. The immediate reaction virtually across the world was one of sympathy: but the changes that then took place in American foreign policy very soon caused considerable alarm in other countries. Securing America was held to depend on hunting down anti-American individuals, groups, parties, nations, wherever they might be found. The rules of military engagement were redefined in the process. It was enough – so the Bush administration claimed – for a nation to be harbouring terrorists, or even any elements hostile to the USA, to make the nation in question vulnerable not just to economic sanctions, but potentially also to pre-emptive military strikes. America and Britain – both powers armed with weapons of mass destruction themselves – chose to wage war on Iraq on the supposition (later shown to be quite unfounded) that it had such weapons and was a threat to world peace.

The irony has been that the policies adopted to secure fortress America have sometimes increased rather than decreased world tension. The fallacy lies in the pursuit of invulnerability in isolation from other fundamental values without which it can clearly not be attained, justice and equity in the first instance. During the last hundred years or so the possibility of material prosperity has grown immeasurably and the actual standard of living of many people has risen dramatically.[15] The luxury possible – for some – is beyond what any ancient Greek or Chinese could have envisaged, not that yesterday's provision is considered luxurious by today's standards.

Yet this increasing prosperity has been bought at the price, first, of a massive deterioration in the natural environment, and, secondly, of the exponential increase in the gap between the rich and the poor – between rich and poor individuals and rich and poor nations. The terms of trade between industrial and developing countries may not have been designed to favour the former, but their effect has certainly been to increase, rather than close, the gap in the standards of living of peoples across the world. Lip service is paid to the spread of democracy, but in practice the myth of democratisation masks the realities of colonialisation, the curtailment, rather than the furtherance, of equality of opportunity whether in the political or the economic sphere. Millions of ordinary people, without any allegiance to the policies let alone the methods of Al Qaeda, feel resentment at what they see as their systematic exploitation by the industrialised nations and the multinational corporations that operate from within them. In those circumstances attempts to increase the physical security of favoured groups, in enclaves for the rich, look like a classic case of tackling the symptoms but not the underlying causes of the problems.

*

Peace of mind has always rightly been prized, but what it consists in and how to attain it are as problematic now as they ever were in ancient Greece or ancient China. Each of our case studies reveals how invulnerability has been pursued, but each suggests some of the delusions of its pursuit. The ancient Greeks had a heightened sense of the frailty of the human condition and of the caprices of chance. But on how immortality is to be achieved, and what kind of immortality that was, they answered with different voices. For some this

109

was a personal immortality, for others just one of disembodied reason, for some the key was purity, for others goodness. Death is nothing to us, some of the philosophers argued, but they offered conflicting grounds for their claims to deliver peace of mind, a conflict that – despite the Sceptics – may well have generated anxiety rather than relieved it.

The Chinese too pursued immortality but of a very different kind – physical, not disembodied. The notion of the eternal life of pure reason was not an ideal that haunted them. We certainly find, in Chinese writings of different types, greater acceptance of the inevitability of change. Although the fate of many great people is tragic in the sense of to be regretted, there was, with that acceptance, less occasion for heroics – where the individual strives, hopelessly, against the inevitable.

The distinctive features that early Christianity introduces include far more elaborate, more concrete, pictures both of salvation and eternal bliss – and of eternal damnation – and a new specification of the conditions under which the former can be attained and the latter avoided. The dispensing of rewards and punishments was now in the hands of an omnipotent and omniscient god – which was most reassuring if you could count yourself among the potentially saved, most disconcerting if not. The message, meanwhile, for non-Christians was that unfortunately their eligibility for the highest rewards was forfeit.

The prospects of invulnerability today, such as they are, are thought to depend not so much on religious belief as on economic muscle. Yet as in the story of Tantalus, the goal still eludes even the very rich – individuals or nations – in that complete security is not now possible without global security. As never before, we are all in it together: the problem of peace is a world-wide one and the solutions must be world-wide too. To demand invulnerability for the few at the price of injustice to the many is self-contradictory. Ironically and indeed tragically, many of the policies designed to attain security piecemeal contribute to aggravating the global situation.

Peace of mind, I shall repeat in conclusion, is a worthwhile value, but in today's world the self-regarding and inward-looking tendencies that often go with it are potentially highly dangerous. That is to say that the egotism that is often displayed in attempts to secure it tends in the long run to make those attempts self-defeating. The message from ancient China, of accepting interaction and of the interdependence of 'all under heaven', seems to provide a more promising framework in which to tackle today's global problems than the exclusive ideals that the West has so often set itself.

5

The Frailties of Justice: Debates and Prospects

If there is injustice, the prospects for well-being or happiness are slim. But how is justice to be attained, within the community, or a state, or between nations? Will it not always be the case that those who can get away with injustice will do so? Was not Callicles, in Plato's *Gorgias*, correct in arguing that might is right? And what of Thrasymachus' claim in the *Republic*? Is it not the case that every political regime defines justice (if it is concerned with it at all) to suit itself, dictators legitimising dictatorial regimes, just as surely as democrats do democratic ones? And what is justice? Can any objective judgement be made on that issue, and if so, on what basis? Or is the search for justice itself chimerical? Does the diversity of human customs and conventions, *nomoi* as the Greeks called them,[1] not suggest that another Greek dictum is valid, that *nomos* is king,[2] and that what will be approved will always be relative to some particular group? But then how can issues between groups be adjudicated? What are the prospects for the just regulation of the relations between nation-states?

Certain conceptual distinctions should be made at the outset, before I tackle the complex and divergent histories of Greek and Chinese thought on these issues and then apply the lessons they suggest to the modern world. First, there is the obvious prima facie distinction between legality and justice. It is true that where the laws are not codified, the question of whether they have been infringed will not be formulated as such, though that will not prevent the question of whether wrong has been done from being raised. But in societies with law codes,[3] there may be provisions that those contain that come to be seen, by members of the society in question, to be imperfect, inappropriate, needing to be revised or even scrapped. In modern states legislative bodies are kept hard at work trying to keep up to date, drafting new regulations to meet new contingencies, including those that arise from new scientific research, such as the possibility of cloning human embryos, or from new technology, such as the internet. Or the law may need changing to reflect changing public opinion, on drugs, or on sexual behaviour for instance.

Then a second obvious contrast concerns the law in the sense of what is on the statute book on the one hand, and its administration on the other. Laws deal with the general, not the particular in all its particularity. So the application of the general to the particular is always a matter of judgement – 'casuisty', in other words, in its original sense. Was the killing in self-defence, or was it murder? How carefully, conscientiously and consistently do the responsible officers, judges, magistrates, elders, perform their roles? How impartial are they? That the laws may need revision is one issue; that those who interpret them may be incompetent or plain corrupt is another. In both cases securing improvements may be difficult.

Thirdly, there is an analogous distinction that is important for us today, though often neglected in academic discussion, namely that of the potential gap between what one might ideally hope for, and what is practically attainable. It is one thing to try to draw up a blueprint for how things should be. It is another to focus on what policies have a chance of being approved, and of succeeding in their aims, in the short, medium or even longer term.

In both ancient Greece and ancient China we can trace major changes, in attitudes, in reflection and debate on the issues, and in the concrete provision of justice. I shall concentrate on archaic and classical Greece on the one hand, and on the period down to the end of the Han on the other.

*

The changes that took place in both the sense and reference of two key terms, *themis* and *dikê*, are eloquent testimony to the shifts in attitude between the archaic and classical periods in Greece. In Homer both terms may be used of customary behaviour without the

114

connotations of approval that go with what is right or just. At *Iliad* 9 132ff., Agamemnon, promising to hand back Briseis to Achilles, swears that he has not been to bed with her, as is *themis* among humans, where that indicates simply what is usual, rather than what is lawful, let alone moral. In the *Odyssey* 4 689ff. Penelope remarks that Odysseus was an exceptional ruler: he never did nor said anything wrong among the people, though that is the *dikê*, the way, of godlike kings – in other words that is how they generally behave. At *Odyssey* 11 218, when Odysseus tries to embrace his mother in the underworld and finds she is an insubstantial shade, she says that that is the *dikê*, the way things are, when mortals die.

In other contexts, however, the positive associations of what is right and just are clear. To describe the Cyclopes' non-human society we are told that they lack *themistes* (*Odyssey* 9 112ff.), that is the rules and regulations and customs that govern proper human relations. In the account of the city at peace on the Shield of Achilles at *Iliad* 18 497ff., there is a scene that describes the dispensation of justice. A quarrel has broken out about the payment of the recompense (*poinê*) for a man who has been killed. On one interpretation, one side says that it has been paid in full, but the other claims that it had received nothing. But on another reading of the Greek, the first party claims to absolve itself by making full payment (in the future), while the second refuses to accept anything. Not only is the Greek indeterminate, but we should bear in mind that this is a description, in words, of a scene that is supposed to be depicted on the Shield. The case, we are told, is being judged by a group of elders, sitting in a sacred circle, and judging the issue (*dikazon*, 506) in turn. Indeed two talents of gold have been set down in the middle of the circle, to be given to the person who gives the straightest judgement (*dikê*) in his speech. It is not explained who contributed that rather considerable prize, nor how it is to be decided who should get it. But the scene clearly depicts more or less formal arrangements used to resolve a case that otherwise threatened to degenerate into feuding and revenge.

Whether human justice, in Homer, was in some way guaranteed by the gods in general and by Zeus in particular is controversial in modern scholarship, reflecting a certain indeterminacy and ambivalence in the texts themselves. At *Iliad* 16 384ff. Zeus is described as sending a violent rainstorm as a punishment on men who 'violently give crooked judgements [or ordinances, *themistes* again] in the Assembly, and who drive out justice (*dikê*), paying no attention to the wrath of the gods'. But as I have noted before, while Zeus is undoubtedly supreme among the gods and ultimately has his way, he sometimes takes his eye off the ball, and can be distracted, as Hera's famous seduction illustrates. But in Hesiod, as we saw, the principle that Zeus rewards the good is made more explicit. *Works and Days* 225f. identifies the good as 'those who give straight judgements to strangers and to natives and do not stray from what is just'. The just city enjoys peace and prosperity while the unjust suffers plague and famine. For the misdeeds of a single man, indeed, Zeus may punish a whole city (*Works and Days* 240). The message is that the cosmic dispensation is in good order. But meanwhile among the humans that Hesiod and his brother have to deal with are the 'bribe-devouring kings', rather different from the elders on the Shield in the *Iliad*. Hesiod is certainly not afraid to criticise them. But the bitterness of his remonstrations and the stridency of his invocation of the eventual retribution of Zeus suggest that he is more hopeful than confident that those in power will listen to him and mend their ways.

Two key changes take place in the early classical period. The first relates to natural philosophy, and the second to the opening up of the whole issue of justice and legality and the relativity of human laws, customs and conventions. From Anaximander in the sixth century BCE, if not from Thales himself, the natural philosophers produced one theory after another, on cosmogony and cosmology, on the fundamental constituents of physical objects and on a whole gamut of phenomena for which they offered naturalistic explanations that had nothing to do with personal gods. Yet while the focus of attention was, precisely, on nature, rather than on human morality, the cosmic dispensations they described are often heavily value-laden and heavily politicised.

Anaximander's sole surviving fragment, referring to certain unnamed opposed cosmic forces, already speaks of cosmic justice and

116

injustice. 'They' (whatever they are) 'pay the penalty [*dikê*: here in the sense of punishment] and recompense (*tisis*) to one another for their injustice (*adikia*) according to the dispensation of time.'

Heraclitus counters with the opposite image and represents the cosmos as ruled by war. 'War is father of all and king of all', he says in fragment 53 – War has usurped the role of Zeus, indeed. In what may well be a deliberate echo of Anaximander, he says (fr. 80) 'one must realise that war is common, and justice [right, *dikê*] is strife and everything happens through strife and necessity'. The paradoxical equation of justice with strife may be taken in one or other of two ways and should probably be read in both, namely (1) what has been called justice, e.g. by Anaximander, is in truth a constant struggle between opposites, that is strife: and (2) strife is what is customary, right, 'just' in the sense we have met before where it refers to what is usual.

Elsewhere Heraclitus goes further and problematises the perspective from which things can be called just. 'To god all things are beautiful and good and just, but men have thought that some things are unjust, others just' (fr. 102). But if that statement seems to open up a gap between a divine and a merely human perspective, another insists that 'all human laws (*nomoi*) are nourished by the single divine law' (fr. 114). The world is a world-order, where Heraclitus is one of the first, if not the first, to use the term *kosmos* in that sense, and physical phenomena exhibit certain regularities. The sun, for instance, 'will not overstep his limits: otherwise the Erinyes [Furies], the servants of Justice (*dikê*) will find him out' (fr. 94). But this order is one of the constant interaction of opposites. If that interaction ceased, the cosmos would end with it (as Aristotle reports, *Eudemian Ethics* 1235a25ff.). The disquieting message is that in the cosmos peace is not the norm, war is.

A further twist is given to the politicised cosmos by Empedocles. His six cosmological principles include two, Love and Strife, that are responsible for bringing the other four (Earth, Water, Air, Fire) together and separating them. They are responsible, therefore, for all physical change and interaction. The implicit criticism of Heraclitus is obvious. The Heraclitean picture applies at most to the cosmos under the rule of Strife. It has its period of dominance, but then Love begins to take over and has its turn. The relations between the two are again captured in an image with legal associations, for they are said to be governed by an 'oath'. In fragment 30 Strife 'leaped up to claim his prerogatives [*timai*, honours], as the time came round which was fixed for them alternately by a broad oath'.

The messages for human behaviour and for the prospects of human justice that can be extracted from this wealth of social, political and legal images in Presocratic cosmology are mostly only indirect.[4] Though many of the images borrow descriptions and epithets that had been used of Zeus, they are now applied to impersonal cosmic forces, not to the wilful anthropomorphic deities of the Olympian pantheon. It is the cosmic dispensation itself that is the chief focus of interest, whether that is described in terms of anarchy, of monarchy or with more egalitarian images. Empedocles is exceptional in that he links the fate of human *daimones*, souls, to his cosmic principles. What happens to our soul in its successive incarnations depends (as we noted in the last chapter) on how we have behaved in this life. The fate of the *daimones* is said to be governed by a decree of the gods 'sealed by broad oaths' (fr. 115) – in terms that evidently echo the 'broad oath' that regulates the periods of rule of Love and Strife themselves.

A general distinction can be drawn between, on the one hand, speculations that focus on the cosmos as such – with more or less prominent implications for human justice included in the cosmology presented – and, on the other, the direct problematising of the nature of human justice itself. That is the second key development in the shift from the archaic to the classical period to which I now turn, and indeed the theme can be found in writings in many different genres in the sixth and fifth centuries, lyric, tragedy, historiography and oratory as well as in the extant evidence for the so-called sophists.

Solon in the sixth century is an interestingly complex figure. He was responsible for constitutional reforms at Athens when he was called in to help resolve the political and economic crises from which it was suffering. That task would, of course, inevitably have brought home to him both questions of practicality and those of justice and equity. Like Hesiod he invokes Zeus as sanction, comparing the swiftness and certainty of the vengeance that he takes on the unrighteous with the sudden scattering of the clouds by the wind in spring (Poem 13: 17ff.). At the same time human responsibility for human affairs receives much more emphasis. It is from its great men that ruin comes on a city – just as thunder comes from lightning indeed (Poem 9). The Athenians should not blame the gods for their troubles: they are responsible for them themselves (Poem 11). The leaders of the people have no respect for justice (Poem 4). As for his own efforts to secure it, earth will, in time, bear witness on his behalf, for he removed the boundary-posts that marked estates that had been mortgaged when he abolished loans secured upon the person and cancelled debts (Poem 36), though he is careful to claim that he 'wrote ordinances for commoner and nobleman alike, making justice straight for each one'. The language of Zeus' sanction continues: but Solon is fully aware that the fate of his constitution rested with the sovereign people of Athens.

Athens was far from the only state where the laws and the constitution were repeatedly contested and revised. But as Aristotle was to put it, *Politics* 1269a19-24, changes to the law tended to undermine the force of law itself. That was Aristotle drawing on the experience of more than a hundred years of intense political conflict and debate. From the beginning of the fifth century, if not earlier, three main types of argument contributed to problematising the nature of justice and the adequacy of ordinary laws, the particular ones of particular states, and sometimes of human laws in general. First there was an increasing awareness of the actual variety of laws and customs (both covered, we said, by the term *nomos*) among different Greek and non-Greek people, leading some to conclude that laws are valid only for the communities that adopt them. Secondly, there is the introduction of the notion of divine, unwritten, laws, to which human laws should, but rarely do, approximate. Thirdly, there is the radical view that laws are created by the weak: the strong will ignore them whenever they can. According to the law of nature, the only law that has a claim to be objectively correct, might is right.

Let me now illustrate each of these themes very briefly, selecting just some of the varied evidence we have for each one.

The topic of the relativity of human customs is brought out most vividly in the story told in Herodotus (III 38) about the Persian king Darius. The historicity or lack of it of the anecdote does not affect its value to us as evidence of the currency of the idea. Darius is reported to have confronted some Greeks and some Indians on the question of how to treat the dead. The Greeks are horrified at the idea of eating their parents' dead bodies (said to be the custom of certain Indians), while the Indians, for their part, are just as shocked at the notion of cremation (a common Greek practice). Herodotus' own comment is that everyone believes his own custom to be the best. Similarly Thucydides notes at one point (II 97) that the Odrysians and the Persians have opposite views about giving and receiving gifts. The Persians considered it more honourable to give than to receive; the Odrysians thought the reverse. From tragedy we may note that in Euripides' *Andromache* (173-6) incest is said to be the practice among some non-Greek peoples and this is not forbidden by *nomos*, while more radically still, in a fragment quoted from a lost play (fr. 19) a character suggests that no behaviour is shameful if it does not seem so to those who engage in it. A naturalistic explanation of this relativity appears in the fifth-century-BCE Hippocratic treatise *Airs, Waters, Places* (ch. 23), when it correlates character with physical constitution and climate, even though it also allows that the political regime under which people live has an influence.[5]

But if everyone had to concede that human laws and customs are hugely varied, the idea that there are exceptions to this relativity also begins to be expressed. Antigone famously insists, in Sophocles' play (*Antigone* 453ff.) that there are certain sure but unwritten laws/customs (*nomima*) of the gods that no mortal can overstep or prevail against (*huperdramein*). She is talking about the obligation to bury the dead – even when the king, her uncle Creon, had forbidden the burial of her brother Polyneices, whom he considered to be a traitor. Although Herodotus often emphasises the diversity of customs, he has Xerxes, no less, say at one point (VII 136) that he will not break the law that holds for all humans, namely that heralds should not be killed. This contrasts strikingly with the behaviour of the Spartans who, we had just been told, had killed Darius' messengers. Thucydides (II 37.3) makes Pericles say that the Athenians obey the law, not just those set up to protect the oppressed, but also those that are unwritten but acknowledged to bring shame on those who break them. Speaking of the need to punish deliberate crime, but not involuntary error, Demosthenes says that 'nature herself has decreed this in the unwritten laws and in the characters of men' (*On the Crown* 274-5).

Finally, the discussion between Hippias and Socrates in Xenophon's *Memorabilia* (4.4.18ff.) illustrates both the widespread acceptance of the idea of unwritten laws and the difficulty of specifying what they cover. The two of them agree that worshipping the gods and honouring one's parents count as such, and Socrates includes incest and is unmoved by Hippias' observation that that is not universally upheld. He is not swayed either by the analogous argument in the case of repaying benefits, for that too is a rule that is often broken. However, the claim, at 4.4.21, that transgression of divine laws never goes unpunished is precisely the point at which – as I noted already in Hesiod – theodicy seems to degenerate into what the realist will call mere wishful thinking.

The third challenge to the scope of human laws came, indeed, from those realists, or cynics, who dismissed their entire basis and claim to be obeyed. Three of the most famous statements of some such point of view come in Thucydides' Melian Dialogue, in the fragments of the sophist Antiphon, and in Callicles' speech in Plato's *Gorgias*, 482c ff.

In the Melian dialogue (Thucydides V 87ff.) the Athenians take a very different line from the one Pericles ascribed to them. Justice (*dikaia*) in human discourse depends on 'equal necessity', that is on an equal ability to compel others by force. The superior will do whatever they have the power to do, while the weak accept what they have to. When the Melians, conceding that they cannot speak on the basis of equal power, appeal to 'the divine', the Athenians counter that they have just as much claim to have the gods on their side. 'Concerning the gods we believe, but concerning humans we know for sure, that it is a necessity of nature always to rule whatever one can' (V 105). In the sequel, the Melians stick to their guns and do not surrender. But when their city has been betrayed and taken, the men are all killed and the women and children sold into slavery.

What we have in the remains of the work *On Truth* (fr. 44a) by Antiphon deals rather with intra- than with inter-state relations. Justice is a matter of not breaking the laws and customs (*nomima*) of one's state. That is glossed as obeying those laws when witnesses are present. But otherwise one should follow 'nature'. The laws themselves are artificial agreements. To break the laws, if you are not found out, does you no harm. But it is inherently damaging to go against what is natural: that harms you whether or not you are discovered.

Finally, there is Callicles' position in the *Gorgias*. Whereas Thrasymachus, in the *Republic*, puts it that each kind of regime sets up the laws that suit its particular interest, Callicles' view is that it is the weak who have instituted the laws – to protect themselves from the strong. Whereas in Thrasymachus the laws are designed to give some legitimacy to the policies of whatever government is in power, in Callicles their function is to curb the strong with talk of shame and injustice if they act selfishly. Yet in reality it is just for the stronger to have more than the weaker. Nature herself shows this (*Gorgias* 483c8ff.), as can be confirmed by looking at the behaviour of animals. Again, inter-state relations make the same point. Xerxes' invasion of Greece, and Darius' of Scythia, were not just by the lights of the *nomos* 'we' have set up, but according to nature – indeed according to the law (*nomos*) of nature[6] – what they did was just.

We find, then, these powerful statements, in Plato himself, of the view challenging the basis of human law and the conventional acceptance of justice. It was, of course, a major part of Plato's own project to counter those challenges. This he did by a combination of arguments, the two most important of which are first to represent human justice as underpinned by cosmic justice, and second to suggest that injustice is harmful to your soul.

As to the first argument, we have already seen (Chapter 4) that Plato postulates a divine Craftsman who, unlike the traditional gods, is totally free from envy. But Plato's picture of the cosmic dispensation does not depend solely on that assertion, but rather on the arguments he gives that the cosmos manifests order, regularity and indeed beauty, a theme developed not just in the *Timaeus*, but also in the *Politicus*, the *Philebus* and the *Laws*, and indeed already in the *Republic*.[7] On this account human legislators should, as far as possible, model themselves on the pattern that the divine creator of the universe provided.

But to that cosmological argument, a psychological one, based on the theory of the soul, is added. The chief consideration that Socrates used, to counter and eventually refute Callicles, is that to behave unjustly damages one's own soul. The analogy with health plays a crucial role here (Lloyd 2003: ch. 6). No one in their right mind would choose to be sick rather than healthy. But just as disease disrupts and harms our body, so wrongdoing introduces disorder into, and harms, the soul – the reverse of what we saw Antiphon arguing. The paradoxical conclusion that follows is that no one does wrong willingly – but only out of ignorance of the dire consequences of wrongdoing on their own souls. Virtue, in the other Socratic paradox, turns out to be knowledge.

The whole argument turns on what happens to our souls: it does not depend on our relations with other people, nor on the harm they suffer from our wrongdoing. Nor is our reputation relevant – for it is recognised that the truly just person is often mistaken for the unjust and vice versa. The thought-experiment with Gyges' ring in *Republic* 359c ff. is designed precisely to bracket any consideration of how others rate you, to concentrate on the state of your soul and its well-being. In the story Gyges, king of Lydia, is given a ring that can make him invisible. That is used to test whether a person is truly just, that is whether he or she would take advantage of the ring to commit injustices, which the really just person certainly would not. Just as we need doctors to restore our bodies to health when they are diseased, so we need legal institutions in the state to restore our psychic well-being. So we should accept the further paradox, that it is better for you, when you have done wrong, to be punished (for your soul will thus be 'cured') rather than, as everyone thought, to escape punishment and get away with it in a life of uncorrected licence.

The argument depends, to be sure, on the contrast between what passes as right and wrong, and what truly is so, in other words on the objectivity of justice and injustice. But there the whole weight of Platonic metaphysics is brought to bear to support the claim that there is indeed a transcendent Form of Justice, which instances of just actions exemplify more or less imperfectly. When it comes to the definition of Justice given in the *Republic*, as each person fulfilling his or her particular role in society and 'minding their own business', that by itself does not tell us very much – but then no more would any verbal definition. When it comes to revealing what the Forms are, Socrates and every character who may be thought, up to a point at least, to speak for Plato in the dialogues are diffident, even though they express complete confidence in the considerations that lead to the conclusion that there must be Forms.

I cannot here pursue further the complex debates on the nature of justice and related issues as they were elaborated, first in Aristotle, through the new Hellenistic philosophies down to late antiquity, though I shall be coming back to some aspects of this in connection with models of the good life in my final chapter. Our next important task is to review the evidence of what actually happened, in the dispensation of justice in classical Greece, first in the relations between states, then within them.

As for what we may call international, or better inter-state, relations, while the Melian dialogue is unlikely to correspond to any actual exchange, its representation of the unrestrained aggression shown by powerful states against the weaker is borne out time and again by what we know of the wars and predations that occurred throughout Greek history. Whether it was Persians or Greeks attacking other Greeks, or eventually Greeks attacking Persians, the main driving forces were self-aggrandisement, greed and what we can even call imperialism, though there were plenty of invocations of just causes and the righting of wrongs, real or imagined. In principle, and sometimes in practice, certain conventions were adopted. We have seen that heralds were supposed to be respected, though the Spartan treatment of Darius' messengers flouted that. The Olympic and other games were periods of truce. The Delphic oracle served as a source of advice on matters to do with inter-state relations, among other things, although its impartiality was sometimes doubted, in some cases with good reason. The Amphictionies (leagues connected with sanctuaries) at Delphi and elsewhere pronounced on breaches of religious codes and could and sometimes did declare Sacred Wars in that regard.

Between states that were more or less equal, or more or less equally exhausted by hostilities, treaties were signed, swearing to peaceful relations for a period, or for 'eternity', and sometimes these held at least for a time. The history of the Peloponnesian Wars is punctuated by such agreements, the Thirty Years Peace of 446 BCE, and then the Peace of Nicias in 421. After the battle of Plataea in 479, the Spartans under Pausanias swore to protect the independence of the city-state of Plataea in recognition of its support against the Persians, although that did not save the Plataeans from later aggression from the Spartans themselves (Thucydides II 71). In 429 the Spartans besieged Plataea on the grounds that it was siding with Athens, from which Sparta claimed it was trying to liberate the rest of Greece. The end of the Corinthian War, in 386, which involved Sparta on one side, Athens, Thebes, Argos and Corinth together with Persia on the other, came with the so-called King's Peace imposed by Artaxerxes II of Persia. Balances of power, as between Sparta and Athens, and later between Rome and Carthage, were fragile and precarious. The best hope for the suspension of warfare usually came from the clear hegemony of one power, but that 'peace' depended on serving that power's interests – and that was what the independent-minded Greek city-states usually labelled 'slavery'. I shall be returning to this basic problem later.

The contrast between the relative lack of institutions to regulate relations between states, and the plethora of them for relations within them is remarkable. Law-codes covering a wide variety of topics begin to be attested from the seventh century BCE. Although some of those held to be responsible, such as Lycurgus at Sparta and Zaleucus at Locri Epizephyrii, belong to legend rather than to history, Solon of Athens was certainly a historical figure, even if doubts have sometimes been expressed about his predecessor Draco.

Our first epigraphic evidence comes from an inscription that dates from the mid-fifth century, setting out the Gortyn Code, though the provisions it contains are thought to go back at least to the previous century. That deals with property, slaves, mortgages, adoption, procedures at trials and many other matters. The very fact that a law code was inscribed is important, even though its significance is partly symbolic. Once that was done, then in principle anyone could check precisely what the laws laid down, even if the non-literate could not do so for themselves.

Eventually in Athens the elaborate provision for the legal system included separate courts, under different magistrates, for different types of case. The Council (*Boulê*) and the Assembly (*Ekklêsia*) tried some cases themselves. The Areopagus had responsibility for certain kinds of religious cases and for homicide, though both its importance and its precise role changed a good deal over time. In addition we hear of no fewer than ten other courts, though not all were operational at the same time (MacDowell 1978: 35-6). These were the Odeum, the Painted Stoa, the New Court, the Inserted Court, the Court at Lycos, the Kallion, the Triangular, the Greater and the Middle, as well as perhaps the most important of all, the (H)Eliaia, the court presided over by the *thesmothetai*.[8]

In Athens, to take our best documented case yet again, there was a distinction between private actions, where an individual had been wronged, and public ones, where the wrong was held to affect the state as a whole. The former were brought by the individuals themselves, who spoke in person at the hearing, though they might have a professional speech-writer, a *logographos*, prepare what to say. Public actions were initiated by magistrates or officials, but they could also be started by private individuals acting, in principle, on behalf of the state. Damages were paid to the state, in such cases, but there were rewards for the individuals who initiated successful prosecutions, and in some instances that could amount to up to three-quarters of the property recovered for the state. This in turn led to the rise of *sukophantai*, as they were called, not 'sycophants' in our sense, but people who brought vexatious prosecutions, denouncing others falsely, generally in the hope of making money in the process. Eventually, to curb such false accusers, fines were imposed on any prosecutor who failed to obtain at least a fifth of the jury's votes.

In a comparative perspective two points stand out, the degree of involvement of ordinary citizens and the principle of equality before the law. As regards involvement, this was, of course, greater in the democracies than in the oligarchies, where the political decisions were taken by a more restricted group, and naturally legal issues could not be entirely divorced from political ones. As noted, at Athens, the Council and the Assembly, which were the bodies that took all the important political decisions, including on the laws and the nature of the constitution, also acted as courts for certain types of cases.

Even though the main courts were under the control of magistrates, they did not act in any way like modern judges. Both verdicts and sentences were decided by the dicasts, who combined the roles of both judge and jury. They often numbered several hundred, and we even hear of cases tried by the entire annual panel of 6000 dicasts. Manning the courts took up a large amount of time of a considerable proportion of the citizen body, and from Pericles' time payment was instituted for jury service. Moreover the dicasts for any one case were chosen by lot on the day from those on the panel who volunteered. This proved a generally effective device against attempts to prejudice the outcome by bribing the jurors, not just because there were often so many of them, but also because no one could tell in advance who the jurors for any given case on any given day were going to be.

This intense participation in the legal and political processes of the state had far-reaching repercussions, as I have already mentioned in Chapter 3. Certainly quite ordinary, unambitious citizens learnt to take responsibility for important decisions affecting themselves and the state. In the courts they gained a great deal of experience in evaluating the rights and wrongs of the cases they tried, in assessing the strong and weak points of the arguments and evidence on either side, in weighing up the honesty and reliability of speakers and of witnesses. The extant remains of fifth- and fourth-century BCE Attic oratory show that considerable ingenuity was displayed in attempts to sway the views of the dicasts, including appealing to their pity by calling on weeping women and children as silent witnesses. But effective as they may have been in some cases, in others we find speech-writers protesting that they will not resort to such tricks. Their line is to congratulate the dicasts on being too experienced and wise to be hoodwinked by such techniques of manipulation, to which they were nevertheless regularly subjected. But of course that line too is also a much used and rather obvious rhetorical ploy.

My second fundamental point concerned equality, and this has to be qualified in two important respects. First, we are talking, as always for Greece, of equality only among a restricted group, adult males who were full citizens. Slaves, foreigners and women had some rights, but not the whole range of those that citizens enjoyed, in particular not the right to participate in the political decision-making process. Secondly, it is also the case, in some of the earlier codes, such as that of Gortyn in particular, that the seriousness of certain offences – rape is one example – varied according to the status of the person against whom the offence had been committed and according to that of the person who committed it.[9]

Yet we must balance those reservations against two other points. First, within the citizen body access to the law was open to all. Anyone could bring a private prosecution, or even initiate a public action as I have explained, just as anyone (understand any citizen again) had the right to speak in the Assembly, the principle of *isêgoria* I mentioned before. Secondly, the basic principle on which all decisions, whether political or legal, were taken was that of one person, one vote.

We take that second principle so very much for granted ourselves that it may be difficult to assess its impact. Defeated parties, if they were outvoted, could not complain, surely, if they had just as much chance to present their cases as the other side. They could live in hopes that they would win the vote on the next occasion, or even get the earlier decision rescinded. I cited before one famous occasion when the Athenian Assembly voted first for drastic punitive measures against the Mytileneans who had revolted against them, and then, the next day, for clemency (Thucydides III 36ff.). But when decisions were thus taken by vote between opposing points of view, there was far less incentive to continue the discussion to work towards a consensus. That is more appropriate in some situations than in others, to be sure. But there are clearly occasions when it is preferable not to arrive at a policy where there are outright winners and losers, but at one that commands the widest possible general support.

One strength of the Athenian legal system was that it was in principle egalitarian, and another is that, as noted, the fact that the dicasts were chosen by lot meant there was less chance of bribery. One weakness that has also been mentioned is that vexatious prosecutions were common. Again, impartial witnesses were a rarity: it was generally the case that those called on were relatives or others with obligations to those who asked them to testify on their behalf. The prejudices of dicasts, and their gullibility, in failing to see through the corrupt informers by whom they were surrounded, are not only satirised in comedy, but denounced at length by Isocrates (XV 15-38). Those who manipulated the Assembly and the courts often themselves complained that those bodies were subject to manipulation, as Cleon did in the Mytilenean debate (Thucydides III 37-8).

More generally a feature of the Greek judicature was what we may call the amateur status of the key decision-takers. You do not nowadays become a judge in any modern Western state without considerable training – which itself may serve to give those who undergo it an exaggerated sense of the sacrosanctity of the existing legal provisions. But in ancient Greece the dicasts were totally untrained – even if many of them acquired in time far more experience than any modern jurors – and they had to rely on their own best judgement on such matters as the precise interpretation of what the laws prescribed. But in the case of recent legislation, they may well have been involved in approving it, if not drawing it up themselves, in their capacity as members of the Assembly.

Miscarriages of justice could and did occur, though of course that cannot be quantified. Socrates' trial for impiety is comparatively well documented, yet it is difficult, or rather impossible, to pin down why things turned out as they did. The motives of his prosecutors were no doubt a mixture of personal malice, intolerance of his criticisms, and hostility towards his assumed sympathy with the anti-democratic cause by way of his association with the likes of Critias, Charmides and Alcibiades.[10] It has been suggested that impiety was included among the charges because after the amnesty of 403 BCE, prosecutions for political offences had been ruled out. Again, Plato certainly believed that the portrait of him as a sophist in Aristophanes' *Clouds* prejudiced the court against him. At the same time Socrates evidently did not help his own case, by what was no doubt interpreted as his arrogance. So far from showing any feelings of repentance, he claimed that his questioning positively benefited Athens. When, according to Athenian procedure, after he was found guilty, it was up to him to propose an alternative to the death sentence demanded by the prosecution, he initially suggested that he should be rewarded with free meals in the Prytaneum, and he changed this to a fine only at the urging of his friends. But according to Diogenes Laertius (II 42), the majority against him for his sentence was greater than it had been for his conviction.

The institutions of the classical Greek city-states are in many respects exceptional. Under Alexander and his successors, and then again under Rome, politics and the law reverted to patterns we associate with central, if not monarchical, government. The dispensation of justice no longer depended to such a degree on your ability to persuade your peer group of the merits of your case. Rather, it was in the hands of officials, magistrates appointed to positions of authority, more or less venial, corrupt or impartial, as luck would have it, but operating eventually, in the Roman case, within the framework of an impressively detailed legal code. Securing justice in private affairs with fellow citizens and others was subject to a different set of hazards from those presented by the mass Dicasteries of classical Athens.

Meanwhile, when it came to regulating the political relations between the Hellenistic kingdoms or between Rome and its neighbours, or again within Rome between competing more or less legitimate contenders for power, considerations of justice generally took second place to those of self-interest and the ability to back those interests with military force.

5. The Frailties of Justice: Debates and Prospects

In the final analysis there is a notable mismatch between the idealism of some of the Greek philosophers, on the one hand, and the real-life situation in which most people found themselves in the Greco-Roman world on the other. The philosophers set down the conditions they thought should be met for there to be justice, and equity at least among the admittedly privileged citizen body. Yet none of that had much impact in practice. Even those who theorised that slavery is an unnatural institution, and that everyone is born to be a citizen of the world, were just that, just theorists. Such moves as were made to abolish slavery came from the slaves themselves, and were a matter of slave revolts, disconnected from the debates in the philosophical schools, and put down with great ruthlessness. Yet if there is the mismatch I have spoken of, any surprise we might be tempted to feel should certainly be qualified. We shall see that the same is true of the next ancient civilisation we have to consider – and of many aspects of our own situation today.

*

As in classical Greece, in the China of the Spring and Autumn, and Warring States, periods there were many independent states more or less constantly at war with one another in their struggles for hegemony or just for survival. But both the total population and the extent of the territory under contention were far greater than those of Greece in classical times.[11] Nor did Chinese states exhibit the constitutional diversity that we find in Greece, ranging from extreme democracy, through oligarchy and constitutional monarchy, to tyranny. Chinese cities were all governed by single rulers, whether kings or dukes, even though they were still nominally under the Zhou Emperor, until that dynasty, which had had no real power for centuries, was finally abolished by the Qin in 256 BCE. At the same time the effective power, in any given city or state, might lie in the hands of ministers, or of nobles, or of particular powerful families, rather than with the titular ruler.

Both periods were marked by hard-fought struggles between states and political manoeuvring within them. First, most of the

131

other states were gobbled up as power came to be concentrated in just seven of the largest, which formed uneasy alliances against any state or states perceived to be a threat to their own independence. Increasingly, these alliances attempted to stem the rise to overall dominance of the state of Qin. But that rise proved unstoppable and culminated in unification under Qin Shi Huang Di in 221. Even though his dynasty proved short-lived, the situation under the Han, which replaced it, was again one of strong central rule, though by the end of that dynasty, in the second century CE, it was much weakened and in many areas of public life order gave way to anarchy.

Texts such as the *Zhanguoce* are full of stories of plots and counterplots, loyalty and betrayal, charting the rise and fall of states and individuals. Many of these, as I noted before, have a covert, indeed often an explicit, moralising message, as they tell how aggressive, unprincipled and self-indulgent rulers came to a well-deserved sticky end. But it is also often recognised that the just and the good do not always prosper – nor do the unjust and evil necessarily get their true deserts.

This provides the background for the very considerable efforts that (as we saw in Chapter 1) Chinese philosophers devoted to offering advice, in general, and to particular rulers, about good order and wise government. The emphasis is not so much on justice as on virtue. The good ruler will follow the pattern set by the sage kings, and avoid those of the disastrous last rulers of the Xia and the Shang dynasties, namely Jie and Zhou, as these were handed down in legend. All were agreed on the need for order, and all saw the good ruler as in tune with the cosmos as a whole, harmony on a cosmic scale being continuous with harmony in the microcosms of the state and of the ruler's own person. The ideal, as we saw, was to follow, indeed to embody, the *dao*.

But beyond these points of agreement, there were substantial differences in the points of view advocated by different groups of philosophers from Confucius onwards. What good order consisted in, and how to attain it, and the underlying questions of whether humans are by nature good, bad or indifferent, are among the most debated questions in classical Chinese philosophy.

5. The Frailties of Justice: Debates and Prospects

The line that Confucius himself took put the emphasis on right-eousness (*yi*) and humaneness (*ren*) and attached considerable importance to the rites (*li*i), that is, not just ceremonial, but the proper conduct of all human relations starting with those in your own family. He is reported to have regretted the introduction of written laws, on the grounds that that distracted people from inter-nalising the principles of good conduct and from practising virtue.[12] With codified laws to consult, they would not ask themselves the more important questions of how they should behave to different individuals in different circumstances, but tend rather to assume that the law relieved them of that obligation and they could concen-trate simply on what they could get away with.

Good social relations, on this view, depended on a recognition of differences in social roles and on a hierarchy of values. In a famous passage in the *Lunyu* 13.18, when a choice is put between family and strict observance of the law, Confucius is represented as coming down on the side of the family. The Duke of She boasts of a paragon of virtue in his state, a son who bore witness against his father who had stolen a sheep. But to this Confucius counters that where he lives they have a very different idea of uprightness, namely that it consists rather in fathers covering up for their sons and sons for their fathers.

But precisely that perception that you should behave differentially towards those close to you and those not so close was denied by the Mohists, who advocated 'concern for all' (*jian ai*).[13] Against the views of the Confucians and indeed of most other Chinese thinkers, and against the grain of Chinese social assumptions generally, the Mohists taught that everyone should be treated equally, at least as an object of your concern. They still thought that the law has to be maintained, and they had some difficult justifying their acceptance of the death penalty for thieves, for instance. There are convoluted discussions, in our sources, of how it is that 'killing robbers is not killing people'.[14] But they redefined several of the key terms of Confucian ethics. 'Righteousness' (*yi*) is defined in the Canons (A 8, Graham 1978: 270f.) in terms of 'benefit' (*li*iii, a term that sometimes carries the pejorative undertones of 'profit' in Mencius) and they added the gloss that the intention is to take the whole world as one's proper sphere of action.

Again, 'humaneness' (*ren*) is defined (A 7) in terms of 'concern' (*ai*, the term used to express the principle 'concern for all', though here, in describing 'humaneness', the model is rather self-love).

Many of those who followed Confucius continued to focus on the virtues central to the ethics of the *Lunyu* – humaneness, righteousness, loyalty, piety, sincerity – but diverging views were taken on human nature. Mencius maintained that humans are instinctively good, but Xunzi thought the opposite, criticising both Mencius and others associated with Confucius directly (*Xunzi* 6). Mencius himself had reported and criticised the view of Gaozi who had held that human nature is in itself indifferent, neither good nor bad. Gaozi had suggested a comparison with willow wood, from which can be fashioned either cups or bowls. To that Mencius countered by pointing out that that involves cutting and carving, using force on the wood indeed. Gaozi's second analogy is no more successful. If you open a channel for a whirlpool to the east, it flows eastwards, and if to the west, it flows westwards. So man's nature has neither good nor bad allotted to it, just as water has neither east nor west allotted to it. But to that Mencius replied by pointing out that water does have a tendency to flow downwards. It can be forced off its course, but that natural tendency remains, just as a person can become bad, but by nature, Mencius claimed (6A1, 6A2), humans are good.

In the continuation of the dispute, in *Xunzi* 23, the wood analogy reappears, though now with the emphasis on the human intervention necessary to make it useful. Human nature, Xunzi argues, has to be forced straight – like crooked wood. But it is inherently bad, requiring teachers and standards to guide it towards the good. Xunzi's picture was a very negative one, of humans in a desperate state until the sages invented the rites and provided models for good conduct.

The emphasis on the need for acculturation agrees, thus far, with a fourth basic position, elaborated by those who were dubbed the 'Legalists', the *Fa Jia*, or Lineage of Law. However, they were a good deal more radical than Xunzi in their insistence on the need for strong government. Han Fei, who had been taught by Xunzi, is one articulate spokesman for this view. In the 'Five Vermin' (*Hanfeizi* 49: 1051) he attacks both Confucians and Mohists. They praised the ancient kings, but for the wrong reasons. 'Benevolence may make one shed tears and be reluctant to apply penalties; but law makes it clear that such penalties must be applied. The ancient kings allowed law to be supreme and did not give in to their tearful longings. Hence it is obvious that benevolence cannot be used to achieve order in the state' (trans. Watson 2003: 103).

One passage makes it seem that, according to Han Fei, the *ru* (here covering more than just the followers of Confucius) and the Mohists are a harmless luxury. The nation at peace may patronise these and other members of the literate elite, but the nation in danger must call upon its fighting men (49, cf. also 50). Yet elsewhere Han Fei argues that these people 'bring confusion to the law' (49: 1057). 'People who deviate from the law should be treated as criminals, and yet the scholars actually attain posts in the government because of their literary accomplishments.' They spread confusion because they do not agree among themselves. 'If you approve of the frugality of Mozi, you must condemn Confucius for his extravagance, and if you approve the filial piety of Confucius, you must condemn Mozi for his impiety' (50: 1085). The trouble is, Han Fei remarks ruefully, that rulers honour them both: by implication, what they should be doing is rather to adopt the moral principles of Han Fei himself.

As I explained in Chapter 1, many Chinese philosophers were much closer to statesmen and rulers than was normally the case in ancient Greece. The Chinese ambition was to make a difference to government. Some were themselves in positions of power and influence. Others who did not hold office themselves, nevertheless offered themselves as advisers. Yet even in the most favourable circumstances, where there was every chance that their advice would be listened to, there was still something of a gap, to be sure, between principle and practice, between what the ideal suggested should be the case, and what actually was. So we must turn now, as we did for Greece, to the evidence for the actual administration of justice.

The public inscription of Chinese law codes begins to be attested from the late sixth century BCE, and like some of the early Greek codes (such as that attributed to Draco) they contain some very severe penalties, not just beatings with the bamboo cane, but branding, amputation, castration and an ample use of the death penalty. We have seen that Confucius deplored this development, but not because of the drastic nature of the punishments, so much as because people might think legal codes might absolve them from the obligation to internalise virtue. Thereafter the dynastic histories and our other evidence record successive, but only partially successful, attempts (often at the start of a new dynasty or reign) to introduce milder penalties at least for the more trivial offences. At the same time there was a steady increase in the elaboration of the law and in the proliferation of its provisions. In the *Hanshu* 23: 1101, we hear that in relation to the death penalty alone, there were 409 articles covering 1882 cases, and that there were no fewer than 13,472 cases of judicial precedents for crimes deserving death (Hulsewé 1955: 338). By that stage there were justifiable complaints that corrupt officials were exploiting the very complexity of the provisions to their own advantage.

Although the changes that occurred both in the law codes themselves, and in their administration, make (as always) generalisation difficult, three points are worth noting especially. First, the emphasis in the codes and in practice was very much on what we should call criminal law. Civil law, by contrast, was very little developed. Disputes between individuals or groups in that area were supposed to be, and generally were, settled by discussion, if necessary by arbitration. If no agreement could be reached between the parties concerned, and the case had to be referred to higher officials, that reflected badly on both parties. The magistrates' chief job was to deal with suspected criminal cases. Both parties to a dispute might find themselves arrested. Moreover arrest was normally expected to lead to a confession and so to punishment.

Secondly, while individuals could be, and were, held personally responsible for their actions, it was commonly assumed, in serious crime especially, that liability extended also to the individual's family. When those suspected of treason or rebellion were caught, it was not just they, but their relatives to the 'third degree',[15] that were punished, exiled, or more often executed. The idea in such instances was no doubt to prevent any possibility of revenge. But the underlying principle of group responsibility was widespread.

Thirdly, the most striking contrast with ancient Greece lies at the point where Greece was so exceptional. In China, as in most societies, ancient and modern, responsibility for administering the law and dispensing justice lay with designated magistrates. Ordinary folk – it is hardly appropriate to talk of 'citizens' in the Chinese case – had no share in that. There was no question of trial by jury, let alone by dicasts who had to settle questions of law as well as determine the guilt or innocence of the accused and then decide the penalty that was due. There were no verdicts taken by majority vote, no sense that your case was being heard by your peer group, but then none of the unreliability of mass juries nor of the unpredictability of their response to attempts to manipulate them. There was no equivalent to Greek-style forensic oratory, although, as I insisted before, Chinese reflections on how to win rulers or ministers round to your point of view without being seen to be doing that were sophisticated (Chapter 1, p. 30 on *Hanfeizi* 12). It is small wonder that the Chinese emphasis was on the virtue of the ruler and of those under him. They simply never contemplated trusting large groups of citizens – the *dêmos* as a whole at the limit – to deliver sound political policies or equitable legal decisions.

*

My forays into ancient civilisations have been undertaken, as before, in order to investigate what might be learned from them for our own situation today. From many points of view we face problems both within nation states and between them that have no parallel in Greek or Chinese antiquity. But if the circumstances have changed, the goals have not. We still seek equity and justice.

Modern states throughout the industrialised world are, in every case, the products of complex processes of development. What each state owes to its past is a complex issue, especially where political revolutions have transformed government, as in the People's Republic of China and in the former USSR. Industrialisation itself poses massive new problems, as does the globalisation of the economy, the opening up of markets on terms that often reflect the disparity in leverage between very unequal partners. The imposition of 'treaty ports' on China in the nineteenth century is just one among many examples of Western economic imperialism. More often the British Empire or the French colonies provided the framework within which aggressive economic policies were pursued, often in the name of 'developing' backward areas and bringing them 'civilisation'.

If we backtrack a little, Western notions of law and justice are an amalgam that still bears traces of a complex inheritance, from Greco-Roman antiquity (from Roman law especially), from Christianity (with its Judaic inheritance) and from other sources, especially Islam, which continued to be such an important philosophical, scientific and cultural influence on Europe down to the Renaissance. I cannot here follow up the elaborate discussions of the different types of law – *ius civile, ius gentium, ius naturale* – and the disagreements about the nature of each, that of natural law especially, that punctuate the centuries from Isidore (seventh century) through Abelard and Aquinas (thirteenth) down to Vazquez and Suarez in the sixteenth and seventeenth. Clearly one fundamental question throughout this period was what law could claim objective status, what law corresponded to God's will. In some theorists, natural law was grounded on the instincts and behaviour of animals (God's creation, after all) but more often the exceptional status of humans (with immortal souls) was marked.

Towards the end of that period the notion gains ground that what is right is so independently of God having willed it to be so. From the late eighteenth century especially the essentially secular notion of human rights has been at the centre of national movements of political reform. Since the Universal Declaration of Human Rights in 1948, that notion has formed the basis of attempts to specify what any human being is entitled to, as a human being, and what International Law and the International Community should, in some way, guarantee. Yet it has to be said that beyond a very basic level, there is no more agreement among modern commentators, about what Human Rights should comprise, than there was in the Middle Ages about what *ius naturale* covered.

The mismatch between the more abstract philosophical analyses and the means available to implement them is as great in modern discussions as I have noted for Greek antiquity. On what basis can a political dispensation be claimed to be just? One recent influential contribution was that of Rawls (1972) who offered as a test the supposition of the 'veil of ignorance'. Let us assume that we do not know what place in society we shall ourselves occupy. Our judgements about the equity of the dispensation in that society will, then, be unaffected by special interests (for we do not know which our interests will be). It would not be rational to gamble on being allocated a privileged role. Rather, it would be wise to ensure that the position of even the least well off is as good as it can be. That principle acknowledged that there will not be total equality between everyone in every respect, but the thought experiment secures far greater impartiality than any individual can normally claim. The veil of ignorance is, in a sense, an extension of Solomon's principle, that where two parties dispute the distribution of goods, one should decide how they should be apportioned, while the other should choose which portion to take.

Rawls and many others have made fundamental contributions to the theoretical analysis of justice, but that analysis remains remote from the real-life problems within and between nations. When we have to decide when the law needs reform and in which direction, the veil of ignorance will cut no ice with fundamentalists who are often the most vociferous advocates of change. Rather, in those circumstances, we must be prepared not to tolerate the intolerant, at least beyond a certain point.

But the problems within nation states generally pale into insignificance compared with those that affect international relations. While the history of changes in the judicature of individual nations has generally been one of increasing sophistication, attempts to set up appropriate international agencies to cope with disputes between states have been notably lacking in success, not so much because of faults in the constitutions of the agencies, as because of their incapacity to implement their decisions.

The League of Nations was boycotted by the USA and failed to act in the face of the rise of Fascism and Nazism. The United Nations, set up after the Second World War, did have the USA as a leading participant, but still suffered from a lack of representativeness, at least until the admission of the People's Republic of China. The permanent membership of the Security Council still largely reflects the outcome of the Second World War, and the exercise of the veto there has repeatedly blocked intervention in conflicts that have threatened world peace. Action was taken, at the instigation of the USA, both in Korea and in the first Gulf War – and of course on both occasions the USA itself provided the bulk of the military force involved. But when the USA has not considered its own interests to be at stake – as initially in the former Yugoslavia – the action taken by others has proved to be half-baked, as the failure to protect the enclave at Srebrenica dramatically illustrated.

The basic weakness is obvious: the UN itself has no means of enforcing its decisions. What is needed is either an independent peace-keeping force responsible to the UN and only to the UN: or else a sense of collective responsibility on the part of the constituent members of the UN, to contribute to the implementing of its decisions, *whether or not* they are thought to serve the member's own interests narrowly defined. The model in the latter case might be more like cabinet responsibility, where even ministers who disapprove, or do not like, certain policies, are obliged to carry them out if they stay in office. We apply that principle in national party politics: the international community has generally not woken up to its analogous obligations.

The provisions to bring war criminals to trial are again in a parlous state. After the Second World War the victors tried leading figures among the defeated in both Germany and Japan. The defendants' pleas that they were only carrying out orders from higher up the chain of command were generally rejected. As Aristotle argued long ago, there are some things that you should not do, even when compelled by a tyrant. Yet many issues of responsibility and guilt remain controversial, and there was never any question, at Nuremberg or in Japan, of bringing suspected war criminals on the victors' side to justice.

Subsequent attempts to strengthen those provisions include, most recently, the institution of an International Criminal Court. Yet this met with the fiercest resistance, both direct and indirect, from the

USA, direct in that they refused to honour their own previous agreement to back the Court, and indirect in that they used the threat of economic sanctions against several nations that did so. The ground for this rejection was that US citizens – who have to carry the chief burden for peacekeeping across the world – are insufficiently protected against possible malicious prosecution. Yet this is in flagrant breach of the principle that the same laws must apply to everyone, to all individuals and to all states, alike. Malicious prosecution is (as the ancient Athenians knew well) a threat that has to be guarded against and resisted. Yet uniformed soldiers cannot be immune to the processes of justice if they flout the Geneva Convention, however hard it may be to bring them to trial and however often in the past they have got away with it. As for nations, no one nation can be above the laws that apply to the rest.

Insofar as the foregoing analysis is sound, the modern world has made little progress over the ancient, one may say, in the matter of the provision of justice. In one respect the situation today is appreciably worse than ever. Even though, for some, with the increase in material prosperity, the threat of destitution is a thing of the past, economic inequality continues to grow exponentially. Massive disparities between rich and poor individuals and groups within particular states have been allowed to grow unchecked – and were positively encouraged by some of the policies of Conservative Prime Ministers and Republican Presidents. As for the increasing gulf between rich and poor states, the developed nations have failed to address that problem in any meaningful way. Grossly unfair terms of trade are not a matter of ordinary injustice, but rather of inequity. The disparities thus created are not just the subject of envy, but also of justifiable resentment. Yet long-term problems are thereby exacerbated in the name of short-term profit, and any politician with any vision should surely see the need to redress the imbalance, if not in the name of equity, then in that of the long-term self-interest of the nation he or she represents and is responsible to.

None of the lessons of the perils of hegemony – not to speak, more idealistically, of its responsibilities – seems to have been taken to heart. Hegemony has to be tolerated by those who submit to it

141

because they have no option. But the more it is geared to serving the economic and political interests of the hegemonic state alone, the less stable the situation. It is in the long-term interests of the USA not to use its position of strength to dictate to the rest of the world what it should do and even think. Rather, the USA needs to pay attention to other nations' needs and opinions, and to the debates and decisions of international agencies. Cajoling the UN and ignoring it if it does not agree with US policies serve to create the very hostilities that those policies are designed to contain. The USA exports the notion of accountability: yet does not practise it in the international arena itself insofar as it does not imagine itself in any way beholden to international public opinion. George W. Bush argued that the issue of taking a second vote in the UN to legitimise the invasion of Iraq in 2003 was a test of the 'relevance' of the UN. That clearly revealed that his idea of 'relevance' consisted in whether the UN would fall into line with what he wanted. The irony, or rather the tragedy, is that the USA claims to be a democracy and seeks to hold itself up as a model political system for the rest of the world to follow. Yet even in the hotly contested Presidential Election of 2004 those who actually voted for Bush amounted only to around 30% of the electoral roll.[16]

Meanwhile, for years, in covert operations around the world, the USA has pursued what the administration and the CIA, but not necessarily the whole of American public opinion itself, deem to be in American interests, whatever the consequences for the democratic process in the countries effected by those operations. As for overt interventions, in the aftermath of September 11 2001, the administration's new policy is that even to harbour elements hostile to the USA may make a nation vulnerable to American military action.

The price paid for what are seen as the bully-boy tactics of the USA is hatred on the part of many, and even resentment on the part of those who otherwise share many of the values for which the USA stands, though many of those nations, including Britain, have themselves often been cast, with reason, in the role of international bully-boy. The hatred and resentment have caused and will continue to cause alarm among US leaders, who are at the same time baffled and themselves resentful of those reactions. For surely the US deserves gratitude, not criticism, from the rest of the world. Yet while the scale of today's problems is new, their nature cannot be said to be. Quite the contrary: for surely some understanding of the quandaries of the USA and of the bitterness felt against its policies could be gleaned from any careful study of the reputation and fate of Qin Shi Huang Di and many other hegemons turned tyrants, or from a reading of the Melian Dialogue.

The ancient world did not have bodies in which world public opinion could be expressed: we must strengthen ours. We need no merely academic debate to clarify the principles that should apply to secure both equity and justice between nations, but those clarifications will be pointless unless we also find the will to set up the institutions necessary to enforce the principles and to implement the decisions our world Assembly takes. Relying on a hegemonic state has never, in the past, proved adequate. It is unlikely to do so in the future.

6

Models for Living

What should be the goals of human existence? What makes life worth living? Many different answers have, in the past, been given, explicitly or implicitly, to those questions. Yet in today's world the questions are often bypassed – as if it were rather embarrassing, even impolite, to press that kind of issue when everyone is so busy being, or trying to be, successful. Is it not enough that you have a house, possibly even two, a car, possibly several, all the most recent gadgets, a regulation size family, with kids that you are going to put through university, that you yourself, and your partner, hold down important jobs and are in line for promotion? If you get a bit anxious or depressed from time to time, isn't that what Valium and Prozac are for? If you face a crisis of self-doubt, when was the last time you saw your psychiatrist or analyst, and shouldn't you see one now? Besides, how can anyone deny that enormous progress has been made, when a mere couple of generations ago, material prosperity, judged even by the now antiquated standards of those generations, was beyond the reach of your forebears?

Some of the ideals that were expressed in ancient civilisations now seem bizarre. The idea that the end of human life, and the primary constituent of true human well-being, should be the exercise of reason, is one example. Although Christianity is still the religion professed by millions of people, the idea that this life is of minor concern compared with the life hereafter (an idea by no means exclusively Christian) is another. One idea that certainly does strike a chord with large numbers of people is the celebration of athletic prowess, but for most that is not an ideal to set yourself, but a vicarious thrill. Otherwise the main Greco-Roman value that survives is the philosophy of *carpe diem*. You've never had it so good, said the

British Prime Minister Harold Macmillan, seeking re-election. The implicit message was, make the most of it, as is the encoded signal of much advertising, where you, the audience, are assumed to be young and prosperous and acquisitive. If you happen to be old, and none too well off, and cynical about acquisitions, try not to feel too excluded. However, the difficulty with youthfulness as an ideal, or even just as a condition for happiness, was always that you cannot approach it, only see it recede. The capacity for hedonism does not increase with the wherewithal to finance it. As for material goods, they are cumulative, for sure. You can see your bank balance, your stocks and shares, grow and grow, whether or not you stop to ask yourself what for, and when is enough? Petronius' Trimalchio had no stockmarket to worry about or gloat over, but otherwise pursued similarly evanescent goals similarly frenetically.

The ancient worlds of Greece and China are not short of individuals or groups who were keen to identify what the good for humans is, and what 'happiness' consists in (though I noted before that, for the Greeks, happiness is no transient phenomenon of your immediate feelings). But in approaching this problem, there is first a particular difficulty with the status of much of our evidence. On the one hand, there are members of the literate elite, philosophers and other writers, who offered moral messages. They gave advice about how lives should be led, whether or not they followed that advice themselves, and whether indeed it was possible to do so in the society in which they lived. On the other hand, there are the values that that society incorporated in its social structures and in the behaviour patterns of those who belonged to it. We too today encounter the problem of the mismatch between what are presented as the ideals for human existence, and the reality of what we have to live with, and the difficulty of suggesting how even a start may be made to move from the latter to the former. That mismatch is certainly prominent in some aspects of our ancient evidence. Then in addition, in between the high philosophising and the realities of existing social structures, there are the implicit values conveyed by cultural icons or heroes, these being not the overt constructions of particular literary artists, so much as the embedded folklore of the culture. Each of those types

146

of evidence suffers from its own shortcomings. I shall endeavour to make the best use of each for the purposes I have set myself here, that of reflecting on modernity from the perspective of antiquity: but I shall not of course make any claim that we can recover, let alone that I have recovered, the whole story where either of our principal ancient civilisations is concerned.

*

In our Greek sources there is a tension between a recognition that humans differ and a belief that if an answer can be given to the question of the good for humans, it ought to be valid for everyone. Many of the moralists, philosophers especially, acknowledge different life-styles – with the philosophers very much tending to place philosophy at the top of whatever hierarchy they imagine or construct. Pythagoras is associated with the topic of three possible motives for attending the Olympic Games – to compete as an athlete (that is, for fame), to buy and sell goods (that is, for money) and as spectators, *theatai* (that is, for wisdom). Our sources report that of these three Pythagoras privileged the last, the life of contemplation, not in the sense of a merely passive reaction to the scenes observed, but rather of an activity directed at understanding.[1] I may note in passing that a fourth reason why somebody might be at Olympia, out of necessity, because you were a slave, does not enter into the picture. Slaves had no choice and they are regularly ignored in such analyses of the motives that may prompt free citizens to pursue the lives they pursue.

Plato in his turn works with different schemata in different contexts. Thus he sometimes allows for significant distinctions between different types of craftsmen, depending, for instance, on how exact their craft is (*Philebus* 55c ff.). But in the *Republic* (581c) he adapts the Pythagorean tripartition, of lovers of gain, lovers of honour and lovers of wisdom. Indeed those three kinds of 'loves' are far from exhausting the rich vocabulary of terms derived from the *phil-* root. Besides the gain-lovers, the honour-lovers and the wisdom-lovers, there are the lovers of sights and sounds, the lovers of the muses, and the lovers of learning.[2] The three main types give

147

him the basis for his analysis of the three main groups in the ideal state. Craftsmen and farmers are lumped together as lovers of gain, soldiers figure as lovers of honour, and philosopher-kings are exemplars of the love of wisdom.

This political schematisation is, of course, underpinned by his theory of the three main faculties of the soul, the appetitive, spirited and rational. There are problems with how these various trichotomies are supposed to match one another (cf. Williams 1973). If the farmers and craftsmen have souls, as they surely do, then they have rational faculties, and that, one might think, might entitle them to a greater say than they are given in the government of the state. Plato argues that while the rational faculty *should* by rights be in control of the soul, it is often overwhelmed by the other two. Analogously in the state, the two other groups need to be controlled by the philosopher-kings. Again, in the analysis of the different types of political constitution in books VIII and IX there are further contrasts, not anticipated in the original characterisation, between royal, timocratic, oligarchic, democratic, and, worst of all, tyrannical types – both of constitutions and of the corresponding human characters. When we are told that the tyrant is 729 times worse off than the king, this is clearly complexity for complexity's sake.

A key issue, however, is just how pure, and indeed self-centred, the life of the philosopher-king is represented to be. The most pleasant and the most worthwhile activity is philosophy, the study of the unchanging transcendent Forms. Yet these philosopher-kings owe it to their fellows to participate in the government of the ideal state. After an arduous training that directs their intelligence to the Forms and trains them in dialectic, they must nevertheless re-enter the Cave: they must go down, *katabateon*, 520c. They were educated in the ideal state: in return, they should be prepared to give up the purest and most pleasant life, which would be entirely devoted to philosophy, and play their part as rulers. Is that being unjust to them? The question is raised: the answer is given, no, and yet the logic of Plato's own argument leaves him with very little room for manoeuvre to justify the claim that his philosopher-kings will willingly give up the highest activity, even temporarily, for the sake of a secondary one.

Aristotle, who shares Plato's view that the philosophical life is the best, has a clearer answer to the difficulty I have just mentioned. Only the gods are able to enjoy a continuous life of pure reason. As humans, philosophers cannot do so. So as humans, we can and should practise the moral virtues, courage, generosity, justice, friendship and so on, participating to the full in the activities of the citizen in the state. Since each of us has a capacity for moral virtue, exercising that capacity has an important contribution to make to our total fulfilment, even though the life of the philosopher as citizen is secondary to that of his activity as philosopher. Again, there are elements of fudge in that Aristotle allows only limited capacities for rational activity to women and restricts the capacity of slaves to obedience. But where the free citizens are concerned, *not* to practise justice (for instance) would be not to exercise an important function of which we are capable.

In Hellenistic philosophy, as I outlined in Chapter 4, the emphasis is more defensive, on the attainment of *ataraxia*, that is on somehow securing immunity from anxiety. Yet both Stoic virtue and Epicurean pleasure cover a range of activities and engagements, while it is still philosophy that you need in order to identify what is truly virtuous or truly pleasant. But whereas Aristotle took the city-state to be the proper locus of human political activity,[3] both Stoics and Epicureans reflect, in a modest way, the changed actual political circumstances that were consequential on the conquests of Alexander and the division of his Empire by his successors. For the Epicureans,[4] the entire earth is a single native land for everyone and the world is a single home. For the Stoics the wise man is a citizen of the world.[5] All human beings should be thought of as fellow-citizens, even though companionship depended on sharing reason, and the actual practice of reason was rare. The ideal of the truly wise person was (we may think) all but unattainable. Certainly practising true virtue, as the Stoics represented it, was extremely demanding. Nor was the Epicurean life of pleasure exactly a relaxed one, since you had always to be vigilant in your assessment of the balance of pleasures and pains.

While the Greek philosophers produced a bewildering array of recipes for the good life, ordinary folk had to get on with making the best of whatever role they occupied in society. If leisure, according to many of the philosophers, was a necessary condition for happiness, that was well beyond the reach of a great many free individuals, not to speak of the vast ranks of the unfree.

Some of those philosophers, to be sure, produced ideas which would, if they had been implemented, have had far-reaching social consequences. Both Plato in his *Republic* and Zeno in his work of the same name (now no longer extant) proposed that wives should be held in common. In Plato's case this was in part for eugenic reasons – there was to be strict control over those who were to be allowed to breed. He also recognised that women are as capable of philosophical activity, and of becoming guardians or philosopher-kings, as men, even though he repeatedly stressed that they are weaker than their male counterparts.

Whether the abolition of the family would have led to an improvement in the position of women in ancient Greece is the kind of hypothetical question to which no clear answer can be given. Women's de facto influence and responsibility were greatest within the home. The chief and fundamental disability they suffered from was, as I noted, in the public, political domain. As Aristophanes' *Women in Assembly* illustrates, proposals that women were capable of participation in that area were, in the eyes of some males, no more than grist to the comedy writer's imagination. Exceptionally talented women, such as the poets Sappho, Corinna, Erinna and others, were recognised and admired, though in some cases, such as Pericles' partner Aspasia, this was with a certain ambivalence. But even when equality between the sexes was advocated – by some male writers, in some respects – that was, in any case, all just abstract theory.

The same applies to those who argued that slavery was not a natural, but a purely artificial, institution. The lot of slaves in practice varied considerably, as between the relatively well-treated household slaves at one end of the spectrum, and the appallingly ill-treated slaves who worked the mines at the other. Against that background, the idea that all humans are equal rings hollow. The Epicurean injunction that slaves should be treated leniently and pitied rather than punished (Diogenes Laertius X 118) had at least some chance of being heeded.

Ancient Greece was a highly inegalitarian society. It is true that the gap between the rich and the poor was, in certain respects, less than it is today. True, there was, in antiquity too, a good deal of conspicuous consumption, but the contexts in which that was displayed were by today's standards relatively circumscribed. Herodotus describes the gold cups and thrones and magnificent chariots of the Persian kings, but even their opportunities for luxurious ostentation do not begin to approach those of the big spenders of the modern world.

The paradox is that in such a society of unequals, the ideal of equality – among the few – was so strongly expressed, and with it a heightened sense of the value of justice. *Isonomia*, equality of rights, was a slogan used by different groups in very different ways. The oligarchs appropriated it for their ideal of each having their (unequal) just deserts, whereby some people were certainly more advantaged than others. But for the democrats, this represented the ideal of equality across the board – though we still have to understand that as stopping short at the limits of the citizen body. Moreover in this case, this was no mere abstract philosophical ideal, but a principle that could be, and was, put into practice in many democratic constitutions in the classical Greek city-states. It guaranteed an equal say in political affairs, an equal opportunity to express opinions in the Assembly (*isêgoria*) and through the voting procedure, an equal chance to influence the outcome. Whatever the imperfections of the actual practice of political decision-taking, and of the actual administration of justice in the Dicasteries, the principle was clear, and could be invoked to help secure justice, right wrongs, and ensure equality within the privileged circle of those who could claim it.

*

From several points of view, ancient Chinese society was as hierarchical as Greek, even though at the bottom of the social pile there were no massive numbers of slaves. In many contexts, in major

151

construction works for instance, such as the tomb of the first Emperor, let alone sections of the Great Wall, the Chinese used conscripts and convicts, where the ancient Greeks would have relied on slaves – not that they built a Great Wall, and in the Parthenon, slaves, metics and citizens all worked together.

But the importance of due respect to social superiors is one of the most commonly reiterated themes of Chinese literature of all kinds. Children should honour their parents, indeed younger brothers should honour older ones, all the way up the political hierarchy, to the loyal devotion that ministers should show to rulers. The conventional classification of people into four main groups (not classes), namely *shi* ('gentlemen'), farmers, artisans and merchants (in that order) does not do justice to the actual complexities of functions and occupations (see Sivin in Lloyd and Sivin 2002: 18). But it does imply a pecking order, even if, as we discussed in Chapter 2, those who were considered to be *shi* varied appreciably over time, reflecting the changes in the social situation from the Warring States to the Empire.

Although in principle there was not much social mobility between those conventional groups, in practice there was certainly some. Lü Buwei, the man who became Prime Minister in Qin and the man who was to complete the unification, was originally a merchant. If in practice he had no difficulty in gaining to access to rulers, this was not just because of his wealth, but also, evidently, because he was as learned as, and no doubt cleverer than, most 'gentlemen'.

But if there are certain similarities in the generally hierarchical nature of both Chinese and Greek society, the ideals for life that were expressed were in many respects distinctive. I discussed in Chapter 5 the disagreements that were articulated on questions of values, notably between the Mohists and others. But now let us return to this theme from the perspective of the question of ideas about what makes life worth living. One of the key notions is, of course, that of the *dao*, the Way, but while most writers saw that as the ideal, they differed very considerably on how to construe it.

An important feature of the notion of the *dao* is that it is multi-faceted, and non-exclusive. I noted before that writers such as Sima

Tan and the author of *Zhuangzi* 33 concede that others had *some* conception of the *dao*, even while they had not grasped it all. Then many recognise a plurality of *dao*s. There can be a *dao* of carpentry, or of butchery, even of thieving – as in the case of the (in)famous robber Zhi, the supreme master in that domain (see especially *Zhuangzi* 29 and 10: 10-15). Of course these are inferior to *the dao*, the one the sage kings embody – at least most thought so, although in *Zhuangzi* robber Zhi ends by ridiculing Confucius' *dao*. But it is certainly not the case that being a craftsman ruled out the possibility of your sharing in the *dao*, in the way that being one was, in some Greek views, incompatible with the proper function of citizenship, let alone with the practice of philosophy.

An absolutely crucial idea, though again one that appears in a great variety of manifestations, is that of the welfare of 'all under heaven', to be secured by good order. When philosophers advised rulers, as they so often sought to do (Chapter 1), their goal was to further the well-being of the state, or after the unification the Empire. That always depended on good government, but there was plenty of disagreement about how to achieve that. As we saw in Chapter 5, Confucius and many who followed him put the emphasis on virtue and ritual and accepted social hierarchisation as funda-mental. But the Mohist slogan was 'concern for everyone'. The same term *li*[iii] was used both by Mencius when he deplored a focus on 'profit' (e.g. Mencius 1A1) and by the Mohists when they applauded the pursuit of what was to the 'benefit' of everyone. Yet while neither before nor after the unification was there unanimity about how to secure the ideal, we should not lose sight of the fact that the ideal was common to diverging viewpoints. To be sure, some stood to gain more, others less, from good government, if it could be achieved: but the focus on what serves to benefit everyone is impressive.

The point can be elaborated by way of an examination of the typical patterns of some Chinese culture heroes. Stories in *Huainanzi* and elsewhere point out that the sage kings of the past were personally and directly involved in bringing about the improvements, in agricul-ture and technology as well as in government, for which they were responsible, exhausting themselves physically, even, in their labours.

Shun taught humans how to build houses. Yu the Great, his successor, tamed the flood, was responsible for land clearance and developed agriculture. In *Huainanzi* XIX 4a the effects of their physical work are spelt out. Yu had calluses on his feet and hands. Before him, Shennong, Yao and Shun were all worn out by their labours.

In general,[6] members of the Chinese elite had almost as much distaste for manual work as their Greek counterparts did (Lloyd 2002a: ch. 4). But the Chinese sage kings were not just models of wisdom: they are represented as performing heroic feats to increase the prosperity of those they ruled. The contrast with the labours of Heracles is remarkable. True, killing the Erymanthian boar was a service to that community in north-west Arcadia. But otherwise his tasks are exemplary for the difficulties he had to overcome, rather than for the benefits that accrued from them. Prometheus was certainly a great benefactor, with his gift to humans of fire and many arts: but for his pains he got, not calluses on his hands and feet, but chained to a rock by Zeus.

Ideals are one thing: in practice the motivations of many Chinese were likely to be as self-regarding as those of Greeks or anyone else. Yet the ideals are worth reflecting on, even if they are just ideals. In this respect, two final features of ancient Chinese ideas are worth noting: first, the clear understanding, in some texts, of the self-defeating nature of the acquisition of material goods, and, secondly, the notion of the value of teaching. Here there are parallels, of course, with Greek ideas – though not exact ones.

Both ideas are to be found in the *Lüshi chunqiu*. In the section devoted to 'Extravagant Music', 5 3 1: 265, we read: 'all men use their lives to live, but do not know what makes them live.' That knowledge – predictably – is equated with knowing the *dao*, but not to understand how one comes to know that is called 'discarding the treasure', and that is bound to lead to disaster. 'Many rulers of the present age regard pearls, jade, lances and swords as treasures' – the list is conventional enough – 'but the more they possess of these, the more their people resent them, the more their state is endangered and the more uneasy is the person of the ruler. As a consequence, he will miss the true notion of "treasure".' The immediate context is the need to recognise and cultivate the right kind of music,[7] avoiding the extravagant music that causes gloom to people and disorder in the state. But the lesson is a general one. Those whose idea of 'treasure' is material goods are dangerously deluded.

The second notable section from the *Lüshi chunqiu* comes in the chapters that are a protreptic to learning. Again the theme of 'honouring teachers' (4 3 1) is developed in standard ways, although it comes after a section (4 2 1D: 196) that contains some rather less trite points about what teachers, for their part, need to do in order to *deserve* honour. 'If a teacher upholds methods that do not transform [pupils] and are not heeded, yet insists that others be instructed in them, is this not far indeed from his desire to have his *dao* practised and his person honoured?' The task of real teachers consists in promoting rational principles (*li*^{ii})[8] and practising morality (*yi*, righteousness). But 4 3 5B: 206 ends with this: 'Thus teaching is the most important element of morality and learning is the culmination of wisdom. The greatest of our moral duties is to benefit (*li*^{iii}) others and nothing is of more benefit to others than teaching. The culmination of wisdom is perfecting the person and nothing perfects the person more than learning .... If one had the influence of a great position, one could use it to rectify all under heaven.' We may note first that even in a paean of praise for education, the idea of good order and of rectifying the world is still on the writer's mind; and, secondly, that education is here the chief vehicle for fulfilling that other characteristically Chinese ideal, of bringing benefit to all under heaven.

The Greeks were certainly articulate in expressing what the individual must do in order to achieve his or her personal *eudaimonia*, though no pagan Greek religious or philosophical idea was a match for the persuasive force of the Christian doctrine of the afterlife, with its twin images, the hope of paradise, and the threat of hellfire and eternal damnation. But the Chinese often expressed a greater sense of collective solidarity, even when certain hierarchical assumptions provided the framework for that idea.

*

But what, I shall now ask in conclusion, is conceivably relevant in any of this for us today? Is it not just as futile to argue a case for self-restraint or for altruism now as it always was? Maybe. But as is clear from the case of the protection of the environment, narrowly self-interested policies are bound to backfire on those who pursue them – as well as on everyone else.

One can learn from the past without wishing to imitate it. There are aspects of both Greek and Chinese values that are worth applying to our own very different situation, even while others no one would dream of applying. Besides, the fact that the goal of further materialist acquisitions is now pursued so relentlessly – and not just in industrialised nations, but also in developing ones, across the world indeed – does not mean that we have to go along with that and give it our blessing, abandoning all critical sense on the subject and refusing to distinguish between the necessary or useful and the merely luxurious or self-indulgent. We need rather to recover a sense of the value of equitableness and solidarity, while not forgetting the lesson that the *Lüshi chunqiu* spelt out, that conspicuous consumption breeds resentment (even while that may also be fuelled by negative feelings of pure envy).

The first lesson that a survey of the ideals of the past may serve to bring home is a celebration of pluralism, and the second and third may be summed up under the heads of countering inequity, and the value and power of education.

The diversity of human talents is well worth celebrating. We have no need to follow many ancient Greeks in attempting some rank order among activities and excellences. To try to prescribe one goal, one ideal for human behaviour, is to depreciate that diversity – unless indeed that goal is stated in the universal terms of cultivating whatever talents you may have: that is true but may be unhelpful. We need not agree with the idea of a *dao* of robbery to applaud the appreciation of the diversity of *dao*s, the multiple manifestations of human creative, intellectual, imaginative capacities.

Yet certain conditions *sine qua non* apply to whatever ideal we set ourselves personally. Stated negatively, the two other lessons that we can take away from the ancient world would be to try to reverse the current trends towards greater inequality, and to counter ignorance and misinformation with education. Both ancient societies we have studied were, I said, highly hierarchical. Some members of those societies were definitely more equal than others. Yet the ideal of equality – within the few – was strongly expressed by many Greek writers, especially under the rubric of *isonomia*, the equality of opportunity in political participation. True, the ancient Greeks themselves did not extend the idea to cover slaves, nor even women in general, but that does not detract from the value of the idea as an ideal. We need to think hard about applying, as well as extending it. It is a question not just of every citizen having the chance – and using it – to participate in the political process, but of there being equality of opportunity much more generally. Inequalities of wealth, between individuals, groups, nations, are not going to be abolished overnight; but resisting their current exponential increase seems a high priority and not beyond anyone's capacity to articulate.

The second defensive ideal comes from those Greek and Chinese writers who expressed their vision of the importance of teaching. Of course when the learned praise learning, that is often mere self-congratulation – and in situations of dire physical need, learning is certainly a luxury. Moreover when defined and controlled in institutions of higher learning (the universities) learning can often be restrictive and exclusive (cf. Lloyd 2004: ch. 10). Overcoming the narrow, inward-looking, trends in some institutionalised education is a challenging task. But the removal of misinformation is always admirable, even if it does not necessarily bring the removal of prejudice in its train. Tragically, much religious instruction seems positively to foster prejudice – but that is not education, but mere indoctrination, and we must be firm on the distinction between the two.

But we may end on a positive note: as the horizon of knowledge expands, we have more and more opportunities to explore the values and ideals that have motivated individuals and whole societies. The 'good life' may take many forms. Ancient endeavours – both their ambitions and their shortcomings – can provide precious insights, not least because they may serve to underline the urgency of our own needs to promote self-understanding, equity and solidarity. Besides, the fact that we are now all in it together means that it is not just altruistic, but in our own self-interest, that we should work not just to understand, but also to counter, the sources of today's malaises.

Notes

1. The Pluralism of Philosophical Traditions

1. Sometimes philosophy was opposed to theology, when the right method in the former was rational argument, in the latter, faith: but in Aquinas, for instance, especially, the two were considered allies, and philosophy was brought in to demonstrate what faith had revealed.

2. Even if several of the many stories concerning the political activities of members of the Academy are doubtfully authentic, the cumulative evidence is impressive. Plato's successor, Speusippus, is reported by Plutarch at least to have been associated, like Plato himself, in Dion's political plans. Hermeias, the ruler of Atarneus, is said to have studied at the Academy and to have had, at different times, other members of the school at his court, Erastus, Coriscus and most notably Aristotle.

3. What follows is documented and elaborated in Lloyd 1996a: 36ff.

4. *Zhuangzi* 17: 81-4 dramatises how Zhuangzi, offered the control of a kingdom by grandees who approached him on behalf of the king of Chu, sends them packing. 'I hear that in Chu there is a sacred tortoise', Zhuangzi says, 'which has been dead for three thousand years. His Majesty keeps it wrapped up in a box at the top of the hill in the shrine of his ancestors. Would this tortoise rather be dead, to be honoured as preserved bones? Or would it rather be alive and dragging its tail in the mud?' The grandees answer: 'It would rather be alive and dragging its tail in the mud', to which Zhuangzi's punchline is: 'Away with you! I'll drag my tail in the mud' (Graham 1989: 174).

5. Nylan 2001 provides an exemplary analysis of the changing interpretation of the 'Five Confucian Classics' down to modern times.

6. It was also, of course, as noted, perceived to be useful in winning arguments in practical contexts (as when Aristophanes represents Socrates teaching how to make the weaker argument seem the stronger).

7. *Shu shu*, literally 'calculations and methods', is, however, far from exactly equivalent to our 'mathematics'. Cf. Lloyd: 2004: ch. 3.

8. The term *tianwen*, literally the 'patterns in the heavens', includes also cosmography and the interpretation of omens: *lifa*, 'calendar studies', comprises other computational work besides the making of ephemerides.

2. Learned Elites: their Training, Openness and Control

1. Although no specialist in this area myself, I recognise that the Mesopotamian materials provide an essential background against which to compare the evidence for ancient China and ancient Greece on the constitution of learned elites. Although scholarly publication of the primary Mesopotamian sources has gathered pace during the last three or four decades and has generated an extensive secondary literature, the importance of this for the understanding of all ancient civilisations is still not fully appreciated outside the circles of Ancient Near Eastern specialists. I wish to record my thanks for the help I have received from Dr David Brown and Professor Francesca Rochberg in particular, though neither bears any responsibility for the use I have made of their advice.

2. Parpola 1993: xiv stresses the complementary nature of the branches of Babylonian wisdom, but Brown 2000: 34 argues that competence in any one field entitled the scholar to be called *ummânu*.

3. Both the date of compilation and the historicity of the materials included in the *Zuo Zhuan* are disputed issues. Sivin, in Lloyd and Sivin 2002: 254, concludes that the work was compiled, by 'persons unknown', 'in all likelihood around 310 [BCE]'.

4. Cf. also Keegan 1988: 233ff.

5. The distinction between prediction of the heavenly movements themselves, and that of events on earth on their basis, is clearly drawn by Ptolemy in the first three chapters of the *Tetrabiblos*.

6. The Dogmatists did not, however, share any particular doctrines. They are called such, usually by their opponents, on the grounds of their commitment to the possibility of giving some account of underlying reality and of hidden causes.

7. Celsus (*On Medicine*, Proem to I, paras 23-4) reports that some defended human vivisection of condemned criminals on the basis of the argument that the anatomical knowledge thus obtained would, in the future, contribute to saving many innocent lives. But others rejected the practice, not just on the grounds that it was disgusting and cruel, but also because it was futile: it told you nothing about healthy living bodies, only about traumatised ones. Cf. Lloyd 1987: 158-67.

8. Aristotle, *Eudemian Ethics* 1247a17ff.

9. Yet Aristotle says that this view was respected more because of Eudoxus' own moral probity than for its inherent plausibility, *Nicomachean Ethics* 1172b9ff., 15ff.

10. I shall be discussing the additional factors introduced by the possibility of publishing on the web in the next chapter.

3. Audiences and Assemblies

1. See Perelman and Olbrechts-Tyteca (1958) 1969, Perelman 1970, McLuhan 1962.

2. These issues have been explored by, among others, Humphreys 1978: ch. 8, 1985, Herman 1987, Ober 1989, 1998.

3. The topic of the relationship between oral and written modes of communication in ancient Greece has been much discussed in recent years (cf. e.g. Harris 1989, Thomas 1992, 1994). For a recent overview of the issues with regard to a variety of literary genres, see Yunis ed. 2003.

4. Cf. also the series of replies on the question of *ren*, humaneness, at *Lunyu* 12.1-3.

5. The *Zhanguoce* (*Intrigues of the Warring States*) was compiled at the end of the first century BCE. Although the accounts of the discussions it contains are fictional, they may be used as evidence of the *types* of exchange that were imagined to take place. See Crump 1964, 1970.

6. By this I mean that it enables greater participation by more people, including in political processes. However, it can also be used to spread anything but pro-democratic messages and is a favourite tool in the hands of terrorists as well as idealists.

4. The Delusions of Invulnerability

1. The idea, with or without the term *phthonos* or its cognates, comes in Homer, e.g. *Odyssey* 4 181f., 5 118ff., 23 210ff., in Theognis (133-42), in Aeschylus (*Persians* 353ff, 361f.), Sophocles (*Philoctetes* 776), and Euripides (*Alcestis* 1135).

2. Artabanus at VII 18 expresses his conviction that a god-sent destruction awaits Greece – which illustrates that such predictions can prove incorrect. Cf. also VII 203 for the idea that the greatest misfortunes strike the greatest men.

3. Cf. also Sophocles, *Oedipus Tyrannus* 1528ff., *Women of Trachis* 1ff., Euripides, *Andromache* 100ff., *Trojan Women* 509f.

4. Long and Sedley (1987: I 144ff.) propose a deflationary account of what the gods are for the Epicureans, namely merely images. 'They are simply the product of streams of images with human shape which enter our minds and form in us idealised impressions of a supremely blessed existence .... By converging on our minds they *become* our gods.' They are 'thought-constructs', then, projections, indeed, of man's own ethical ideals.

5. Long and Sedley 1987: Sections 1-3, 68-70 and 71-2, set out the main sources for early (fourth-century BCE) Pyrrhonism, for the Scepticism practised in the Academy under Carneades and others, and for the first- and second-century CE revival of Pyrrhonism, respectively.

6. The main Stoic exception is Posidonius, whose contributions are, however, particularly difficult to reconstruct, given the loss of all his main writings.

7. I have discussed this issue in general in Lloyd 1990, and in relation to Galen in particular in Lloyd 1996b.

8. Thus *Huainanzi* XVIII 3b-4a follows this general schema in detailing the downfall of Duke Li of Jin. Yet XVIII 26a in the same work notes that there are many who have lost kingdoms despite having practised virtue.

9. This is a recurrent theme in the case-histories of Chunyu Yi in *Shiji* 105. Cf. Hsu 2002.

10. See for example *Lunyu* 1.1, 1.16, and the more general claims for imperturbability at 6.11, 7.16, 12.4, and 14.28. But at 14.30, 15.19, the true gentleman is said to be concerned about his own abilities and at 15.20 at the prospect of not leaving behind a reputation when he dies. When the *Lüshi chunqiu* discusses invulnerability, it does so primarily in terms of a person whose honour remains intact, even though he may be insulted (see 12.5.4: 641, Knoblock and Riegel 2000: 269ff.).

11. Some have argued that the two terms *hun* and *po* reflect dualist beliefs where, on separation from the body after death, *hun* goes to heaven and *po* to earth. But in a critical re-evaluation of the evidence, including that from grave stelai, Brashier 1996 has cast doubt on this and pointed out, for instance, that the departure of *hunpo* does not necessarily bring about death, and *hunpo* deficiency is associated with ill-health. As regards the relations between humans and spirits, *shen*, Puett 2002: ch. 3 has recently contrasted the different stances taken in works of different periods, pre-imperial and imperial, with some texts insisting on the gap between those two, while others allowing the possibility of humans becoming spirits. Cf. Loewe 1982: ch. 3, Harper 1998: 396, 411, Poo 1998: ch. 7. On the disputed issue of 'shamanism' in China, contrast Puett 2002: ch. 3 and Graham 1989: 100ff.

12. In *Zhuangzi* 18: 15-19, Zhuangzi is represented as not mourning his own wife's death – thought shocking behaviour by his friend Hui Shi. But Zhuangzi explains his wife's being born and dying as parallel to the changing seasons: 'this is to be companion with spring and autumn, summer and winter, in the procession of the four seasons' (Graham 1989: 175).

13. There are references in classical Chinese texts (for instance *Mozi* ch. 25: 53) to the need to conduct sacrifices to the Lord on High and to the spirits correctly, and if that is not done, you should expect to be punished. But that is retribution for non-fulfilment of ordinary human duties, not divine envy of particular human good fortune.

14. See Chapter 5, p. 134.

15. Among the modern rich, considerable resources are expended on attempts to prolong life or at least to slow the natural processes of degeneration, which share, in different circumstances, the vanity of some of the ancient Chinese obsessions with macrobiotics.

5. The Frailties of Justice: Debates and Prospects

1. The term *nomos* covered legal provisions as well as customs and conventions, but these three are often run together and it becomes arbitrary to translate in terms of one of those concepts to the exclusion of the other two.

2. As in Pindar, fr. 169a. This is cited in Herodotus III 38 to show that people follow their own customs for preference, but it is also quoted, and the interpretation twisted, by Callicles in Plato's *Gorgias* 484b to support his view that might is right (see p. 122). Pindar's own position has been the subject of vigorous controversy, but it is clear that for him *nomos* does not just cover human laws/customs/conventions for it is said to hold sway also over immortals.

3. Many early law-codes, such as that of Hammurabi, are models or ideals, not practical provisions to be applied as they stand. From the immense literature on the subject, Diamond 1971 stands out as a particularly lucid discussion, and cf. Westbrook 1988 and Roth 1995.

4. Lloyd 1966 undertakes a detailed discussion of political and legal images in Presocratic cosmology.

5. Elsewhere, in ch. 14, *Airs, Waters, Places* cites the case of the Macrocephaloi moulding the heads of their children to illustrate how what may start off as a custom can cause changes in a population's physique that then become part of their nature.

6. The expression 'law of nature' here is a deliberate oxymoron and has, of course, nothing to do with laws of nature as we understand that expression in science.

7. See for example *Republic* 530a, *Politicus* 269d ff., *Philebus* 28c ff., *Timaeus* 28a ff., 30a and *Laws* 902e.

8. The term (H)Eliaia was also sometimes used for courts in general.

9. Thus at Gortyn, there are six different categories of rape, with penalties ranging from 200 staters (2400 obols) when the rape is committed by a slave against a free person, to a mere one obol, in certain cases of rape committed against household slaves. The penalty for adultery varied not just with who committed it, but also where. See Willetts 1967: 10 and 40.

10. Critias was the leader of the Thirty Tyrants who conducted a coup in 404, Charmides was one of the Ten who ruled in Piraeus in association with the Thirty, and Alcibiades' loyalty to Athens was repeatedly called into question (in 414 he actually defected to Sparta).

11. In a recent contribution to a volume devoted to the comparative study of city-states, Lewis (2000) has examined the archaeological evidence that confirms that there were large numbers of cities in China during the Spring and Autumn periods. Many of these were quite small and appear to have enjoyed a considerable extent of autonomy, even though they were nominally under the rule of the Zhou kings. Lewis further points out that Chinese rulers normally depended on the agreement not just of the nobles but also of their populations to implement the policies they adopted and that there are cases where their wishes were blocked, and even some where they were themselves removed from power, by the inhabitants of their cities. Yet it seems that at no point did the common people attempt to rule as a group. The absence of alternative forms of government stands out as the main point of contrast with ancient Greece.

12. See *Zuo Zhuan*, Zhao 29, Graham 1989: 276.

13. See especially *Mozi* chs 14-16 and 44 (*daqu*) ('Expounding the Canons' 6, Graham 1989: 156ff.).

14. See especially *Mozi* ch. 45 (*xiaoqu*) ('Names and Objects' 15, Graham 1989: 151f.).

15. On one interpretation, this meant the members of all three clans, the father's, the mother's and the wife's.

16. There is a brief critique of the actual workings of democracy in the USA and the UK in Lloyd 2004: ch. 12.

6. Models for Living

1. Cicero, *Tusculan Disputations* V 3 8-9, cites Heracleides for this, and cf. Diogenes Laertius VIII 8.

2. The compounds of *phil-* include *philochrêmatos, philokerdês, philotimos, philonikos, philotheamones, philêkooi, philosophoi, philologoi, philomousoi, philomatheis*, and others I do not mention in my text, such as *philotechnoi* (lovers of arts/crafts), *philothêroi* (lovers of hunting), *philoponoi* (lovers of labour), *philodoxoi* (lovers of opinion), *philogumnastikê* (love of athletics). The *Republic* on its own is an almost inexhaustible source for Plato's ideas about, and criticisms of, models for living.

3. When he defined humans as *politika zôa* – polis-dwelling animals – it was indeed in the *polis* that they should exercise that function, even though he was well aware that many humans do not, in fact, live in anything like city-states.

4. See Diogenes of Oenoanda, 30 II 3-11.

5. See, for example, Plutarch, *On the Fortune of Alexander* ch. 6: 329a-b, and other texts collected in Long and Sedley 1987: section 67. Already in the fifth century BCE the philosopher Anaxagoras is said to have considered 'the heavens' as his 'home country' (Diogenes Laertius II 7).

6. However, *Zhuangzi* 33: 27-9 implies that Mo Di and his followers did (foolishly, in this author's view) wear themselves out just like Yu, taking him as their model.

7. The same graph read as *yue* means music, when read as *yao* means pleasure, and as *le*, happiness. The chief context in this chapter is, however, music.

8. This is the *li*[ii] that denotes pattern or order, to be contrasted with *li*[iii] used below with the meaning 'benefit', but by Mencius, as explained, in the sense of profit.

Glossary of Chinese Terms

I list below some of the more important or problematic Chinese terms, the translations I have used and the passages where their meaning is explicated.

ai	愛	concern, p. 134
boshi	博士	erudites, scholars of broad learning, pp. 28, 30, 41-2, 76
dao	道	the way, pp. 23-6, 33, 43, 87, 102, 105, 132, 152-6
fa jia	法家	lineage of law, Legalists, p. 134
gui	鬼	ghosts, p. 102
hunpo	魂魄	soul: spiritual aspects of humans, pp. 102, 162n.11
jia	家	family, lineage, p. 47
jian ai	兼愛	concern for everyone, p. 133
jing	經	canons, p. 47
ke	客	guests, p. 27
li^i	禮	rites, p. 133
li^{ii}	理	ritual principles, p. 155
li^{iii}	利	profit, benefit, pp. 133, 153, 155, 164n.8
lifa	曆法	calendrical studies, pp. 30, 43, 159n.8
qi	氣	breath, energy, p. 25
ren	仁	humaneness, pp. 133-4, 161n.4
ru	儒	'Confucian', member of literate elite, pp. 23-4, 41-2, 56, 135
shen	神	spirit, daemonic, pp. 102, 162n.11
shenming	神明	illumination, p. 102
shi	士	'gentleman', pp. 41-2, 152
shu shu	數術	calculations and methods, pp. 30, 159n.7
tai xue	太學	Grand (Imperial) Academy, p. 44
tianwen	天文	heavenly patterns, pp. 30, 43, 159n.8
wu wei	無為	non intervention, no ado, pp. 26-7, 80, 102-3
xian	仙	immortal, p. 102
xue	學	learning, p. 22
yi	義	righteousness, pp. 133, 155
yin yang	陰陽	negative and positive principles, pp. 23, 25, 30, 87, 104
youshui	遊說	itinerant advisers, pp. 30, 75
yue	樂	music, p. 164n.7
zhengming	正名	rectification of names, p. 29
zhexue	哲學	'philosophy', p. 22

Notes on Editions

For Greek and Latin texts I use the editions specified in the third edition of *The Oxford Classical Dictionary* (ed. S. Hornblower and A. Spawforth, Oxford 1996).

For the Chinese dynastic histories (*Hanshu, Hou Hanshu, Shiji*) I use the standard *Zhonghua shuju* editions. For philosophical texts I use the Harvard Yenching Institute series editions of *Mengzi, Mozi, Xunzi, Zhuangzi*, and the University of Hong Kong Institute of Chinese Studies series editions of *Lunyu, Yijing, Zhanguoce*. For the *Huangdi neijing lingshu* recension I use the edition of Ren Yingqiu (Beijing 1986). For the mathematical texts, *Jiuzhang suanshu* and *Zhoubi suanjing* I use the edition of Qian Baocong, *Suanjing shishu* (Beijing 1963).

I cite other texts by the following editions:

Hanfeizi in the edition of Chen Qiyou (Shanghai 1958).
Huainanzi in that of Liu Wendian (Shanghai 1923).
Lunheng in that of Liu Pansui (Beijing 1957).
Lüshi chunqiu in that of Chen Qiyou (Shanghai 1984) using the section subdivisions in Knoblock and Riegel 2000.
Zuozhuan in the edition of Yang Bojun, 4 vols (Beijing 1981) cited by Duke and Year.

References

Barton, T. (1994) *Ancient Astrology* (London).

Bielenstein, H. (1980) *The Bureaucracy of Han Times* (Cambridge).

Brashier, K.E. (1996) 'Han Thanatology and the Division of "Souls" ', *Early China* 21: 125-58.

Brinkman, J.A. (1990) 'The Babylonian Chronicle Revisited', in *Lingering Over Words*, ed. T. Abusch, J. Huehnergard, P. Steinkeller (Atlanta, Georgia), pp. 73-104.

Brown, D. (2000) *Mesopotamian Planetary Astronomy-Astrology* (Groningen).

Burnyeat, M.F. ed. (1983) *The Skeptical Tradition* (Berkeley).

Crump, J.I. (1964) *Intrigues: Studies of the Chan-Kuo Ts'e* (Ann Arbor).

—— (1970) *Chan-Kuo Ts'e* (Oxford).

Csikszentmihalyi, M. and Nylan, M. (2003) 'Constructing Lineages and Inventing Traditions Through Exemplary Figures in Early China', *T'oung Pao* 89: 59-99.

Cullen, C. (2000) 'Seeing the Appearances: Ecliptic and Equator in the Eastern Han', *Studies in the History of Natural Sciences* 19: 352-82.

Dawson, R. (1994) *Sima Qian: Historical Records* (Oxford).

Detienne, M. ed. (2003) *Qui veut prendre la parole?* (Paris).

—— and Vernant, J.P. (1978) *Cunning Intelligence in Greek Culture and Society*, trans. J. Lloyd of *Les ruses de l'intelligence: La mètis des grecs* (Paris, 1974) (Hassocks).

Diamond, A.S. (1971) *Primitive Law Past and Present* (London).

Elman, B. (2000) *A Cultural History of Civil Examinations in Late Imperial China* (Berkeley).

Fales, F.M. and Postgate, J.N. (1992) *Imperial Administrative Records, Part I* (State Archives of Assyria 7, Helsinki).

Frede, M. (2004) 'Aristotle's Account of the Origins of Philosophy', *Rhizai* 1: 9-44.

Graham, A.C. (1978) *Later Mohist Logic, Ethics and Science* (London).

—— (1989) *Disputers of the Tao* (La Salle, Illinois).

Harper, D.J. (1998) *Early Chinese Medical Literature: the Mawangdui Medical Manuscripts* (London).

Harris, W.V. (1989) *Ancient Literacy* (Cambridge, MA).

Herman, G. (1987) *Ritualised Friendship and the Greek City* (Cambridge).

Hsu, E. (2002) *The Telling Touch* (Habilitationschrift, Sinology, University of Heidelberg).

Hucker, C.O. (1985) *A Dictionary of Official Titles in Imperial China* (Stanford).

Hulsewé, A.F.P. (1955) *Remnants of Han Law*, vol. 1: *Introductory Studies* (Leiden).

Humphreys, S.C. (1978) *Anthropology and the Greeks* (London).
—— (1985) 'Social Relations on Stage: Witnesses in Classical Athens', *History and Anthropology* 1: 313-69.
Keegan, D. (1998) *The Huang-ti nei-ching. The Structure of the Compilation, the Significance of the Structure*, unpublished PhD. dissertation, University of California, Berkeley.
Kirk, G.S., Raven, J.E. and Schofield, M. (1983) *The Presocratic Philosophers*, 2nd edn (1st edn 1957) (Cambridge).
Knoblock, J. (1988-94) *Xunzi: A Translation and Study of the Complete Works*, 3 vols (Stanford).
—— and Riegel, J. (2000) *The Annals of Lü Buwei* (Stanford).
Laks, A. (2002) ' "Philosophes Présocratiques": Remarques sur la construction d'une catégorie de l'historiographie philosophique', in *Qu'est-ce que la philosophie présocratique?* ed. A. Laks and C. Louguet (Lille), pp. 17-38.
Lambert, W.G. (1967) 'Enmeduranki and Related Matters', *Journal of Cuneiform Studies* 21: 126-38.
Lewis, M.E. (2000) 'The City-State in Spring-and-Autumn China', in *A Comparative Study of Thirty City-State Cultures*, ed. M.H. Hansen (Copenhagen), pp, 359-73.
Lloyd, G.E.R. (1966) *Polarity and Analogy* (Cambridge).
—— (1979) *Magic Reason and Experience* (Cambridge).
—— (1987) *The Revolutions of Wisdom* (Berkeley).
—— (1990) *Demystifying Mentalities* (Cambridge).
—— (1996a) *Adversaries and Authorities* (Cambridge).
—— (1996b) 'Theories and Practices of Demonstration in Galen', in *Rationality in Greek Thought*, ed. M. Frede and G. Striker (Oxford), pp. 255-77.
—— (2002a) *The Ambitions of Curiosity* (Cambridge).
—— (2002b) 'Le pluralisme de la vie intellectuelle avant Platon', in *Qu'est-ce que la philosophie présocratique?*, ed. A. Laks and C. Louguet (Lille), pp. 39-53.
—— (2003) *In the Grip of Disease: Studies in the Greek Imagination* (Oxford).
—— (2004) *Ancient Worlds, Modern Reflections* (Oxford).
—— and Sivin, N. (2002) *The Way and the Word* (New Haven).
Lloyd-Jones, H. (1983) *The Justice of Zeus* 2nd edn (1st edn 1971) (Berkeley).
Loewe, M.A.N. (1982) *Chinese Ideas of Life and Death* (London).
Long, A.A. and Sedley, D.N. (1987) *The Hellenistic Philosophers*, 2 vols (Cambridge).
MacDowell, D.M. (1978) *The Law in Classical Athens* (London).
McLuhan, H.M. (1962) *The Gutenberg Galaxy* (London).
Mansfeld, J. (1990) *Studies in the Historiography of Greek Philosophy* (Assen).
Nutton, V. (1988) *From Democedes to Harvey* (London).
Nylan, M. (2001) *The Five 'Confucian' Classics* (New Haven).
Ober, J. (1989) *Mass and Elite in Democratic Athens* (Princeton).
—— (1998) *Political Dissent in Democratic Athens: Intellectual Critics of Popular Rule* (Princeton).

References

Oppenheim, A.L. (1969) 'Divination and Celestial Observation in the Last Assyrian Empire', *Centaurus* 14: 97-135.

Parpola, S. (1993) *Letters from Assyrian and Babylonian Scholars* (State Archives of Assyria 10, Helsinki).

Perelman, C. (1970) *Le Champ de l'argumentation* (Brussels).

—— and Olbrechts-Tyteca, L. (1969) *The New Rhetoric*: *A Treatise on Argumentation*, trans. J. Wilkinson and P. Weaver of *La nouvelle rhétorique* (Paris, 1958) (Notre Dame).

Poo Mu-chou (1998) *In Search of Personal Welfare: A View of Ancient Chinese Religion* (Albany).

Popkin, R.H. (1979) *The History of Skepticism from Erasmus to Spinoza*, 2nd edn (1st edn 1964) (Berkeley).

Puett, M. (2002) 'Humans and Gods: The Theme of Self-Divinization in Early China and Early Greece', in *Early China/Ancient Greece: Thinking Through Comparisons*, ed S. Shankman and S.W. Durrant (Albany), ch. 3: 55-74.

Rawls, J. (1972) *A Theory of Justice* (Oxford).

Rochberg, F. (2000) 'Scribes and Scholars: the *tupšar Enūma Anu Enlil*', in *Assyriologica et Semitica*, ed J. Marzahn and H. Neumann (Alter Orient und Altes Testament, 252, Münster), pp. 359-75.

—— (2004) *The Heavenly Writing: Divination, Horoscopy and Astronomy in Mesopotamian Culture* (Cambridge).

Roth, M.T. (1995) *Law Collections from Mesopotamia and Asia Minor* (Atlanta).

Sivin, N. (1968) *Chinese Alchemy: Preliminary Studies* (Cambridge, MA).

—— (1995a) 'The Myth of the Naturalists', in *Medicine, Philosophy and Religion in Ancient China* (Aldershot), ch. IV.

—— (1995b) 'Text and Experience in Classical Chinese Medicine', in *Knowledge and the Scholarly Medical Traditions*, ed. D. Bates (Cambridge), pp. 177-204.

Thomas, R. (1992) *Literacy and Orality in Ancient Greece* (Cambridge).

—— (1994) 'Literacy and the City-State in Archaic and Classical Greece', in *Literacy and Power in the Ancient World*, ed. A.K. Bowman and G. Woolf (Cambridge), pp. 33-50.

Too, Yun Lee (1995) *The Rhetoric of Identity in Isocrates* (Cambridge).

Watson, B. (2003) *Han Feizi: Basic Writings,* 2nd edn (1st edn 1964) (New York).

Westbrook, R. (1988) *Studies in Biblical and Cuneiform Law* (Cahiers de la Revue Biblique 26, Paris).

Willetts, R.F. (1967) *The Law Code of Gortyn* (Berlin).

Williams, B.A.O. (1973) 'The Analogy of City and Soul in Plato's *Republic*', in *Exegesis and Argument*, ed. E.N. Lee, A.P.D. Mourelatos and R.M. Rorty (Assen), pp. 196-206.

Wittgenstein, L. (1953) *Philosophical Investigations* (Oxford).

Yunis, H. ed. (2003) *Written Texts and the Rise of Literate Culture in Ancient Greece* (Cambridge).

Index

173